Sort My Money

Your 12-step money makeover to a better life

David Rankin

Published in 2014

This book does not offer personalised legal or financial advice. The author and the publisher expressly disclaim any liability, risk or loss incurred as a result, either directly or otherwise, of the usage and application of any part of this work.

Copyright © 2014 David Rankin

All rights reserved. No part of this publication may be reproduced, stored or transmitted in any form or by any means without the prior written permission of the copyright holder.

ISBN: 1500747262
ISBN 13: 9781500747268
Library of Congress Control Number: 2014914550
CreateSpace Independent Publishing Platform
North Charleston, South Carolina

For Tanja, my ever-supportive wife

"The most difficult thing is the decision to act. The rest is merely tenacity. The fears are paper tigers. You can do anything you decide to do. You can act to change and control your life…The process is its own reward."

Amelia Earhart, the pioneering aviator—the first woman to fly solo across the Atlantic Ocean.

Table of Contents

FOREWORD ix

STEP 1: CHOOSING OUR DESTINATION
Setting our Goals 1

STEP 2: THE STARTING POINT OF OUR JOURNEY
Our Current Financial Situation 8

STEP 3: OUR MEANS OF TRANSPORT
The Power of a Budget 15

STEP 4: REBUILDING OUR ENGINE
Drawing up our Budget 27

STEP 5: HITTING THE ROAD
Starting to Live by a Budget 47

STEP 6: DRIVING THE DRIVE
Spending Cash   56

STEP 7: THE STAGES OF OUR JOURNEY
Financial Stepping Stones   69

STEP 8: PICKING UP SPEED
Gaining Financial Momentum   82

STEP 9: AVOIDING WRONG TURNS
Preventing Financial Pitfalls   91

STEP 10: GOING IT ALONE
Personal Budgeting Makes Business Sense   104

STEP 11: FILLING THE TANK
Boosting our Income   118

STEP 12: "OH, THE PLACES YOU'LL GO!"
The Life your Budget Will Help you Create   127

Foreword

When I was a boy, my father had a book about microchips. The front cover featured a silicon chip superimposed on a fingernail.

At the time, he told me that these tiny electronic circuits (which are now on course to become invisible to the human eye) were set to change the world.

Occasionally, I think back to his prophetic words. When a satellite-powered app shows me the way to a new destination. When I track down a long-lost friend on social media within seconds. When I tune in to breaking news from half way around the planet on my smartphone.

Microchip technology has transformed our existence, created new life choices and empowered us in ways we could not have foreseen.

And so it is with our money. When we actively gain control of it and harness its enormous potential, the transformative and empowering effect on our lives is beyond anything we could have imagined.

Finances that start to obey our wishes are nothing short of a revelation; one which inspires ever more ambitions that would have been unthinkable before our money makeover.

It was only when I moved on from a career in banking to become a financial coach that I began to witness this turn-around in my customers' lives. A change that comes about when they are given the skills they need to take complete charge of their money and to channel its power. After which, they never look back.

In nearly every case, and utterly regardless of rich or poor, there is an aha-moment. An eye-opening realisation that not only does this path of total financial control actually exist, but that it is fulfilling and enriching beyond anything they have ever experienced.

Hence my decision to write a book in which I have broken down this roadmap to financial success into 12 simple steps. My way of making this 'road less travelled' accessible to all who wish to venture there.

Step 1:

Choosing Our Destination

Setting our Goals

Life is a journey.
It is an idea most of us subscribe to in theory, but few of us live out in practice.

When we set off on a holiday, we know where we are going and where the next destination is—be it the airport or the hotel—because the trip is planned in advance and executed according to that plan. It happens because it's planned.

Yet, for many of us, this proactive journey does not really happen. Rather, we end up drifting on the ocean of life. We find ourselves in unexpected places which, more often than not, we do not really like, but we end up staying there anyway.

Obviously, any journey requires some degree of flexibility, but a journey without a plan is a permanent magical mystery tour, with the novelty being very short lived.

Our finances are the engine of this journey. If we neglect them, they break down, splutter along or never fire on all cylinders, thereby constraining the breadth and quality of our life experience.

This book is about changing all of that. It is about the optimisation and ongoing maintenance of our financial engine, which will then reward us by taking us on an amazing journey of life that we had never thought possible.

Fresh Start

If your finances are taking you nowhere and your life is stuck in a rut, this is your second chance; your opportunity to press reset.

Just as a travel story is not about the engine that enables the trip, so this book is not primarily about money. If money plays the lead part in your own life story, and if all of your spare energy is spent in maintaining it, this information will help you bring about the change of roles that you require.

By systemising our finances, we transform the relationship we have with them. We go from being at the mercy of our money to becoming the master of our money. We transition from order taker to order giver. Money, that we used to perceive as a tyrant, now becomes our liberator.

On the basis that a journey has many destinations—each one propelling us to the next—we start small, but we are encouraged to dream big. Today is the day we begin our financial journey afresh.

Anything is possible if we set out with a plan, a map of our life journey, and stick to the route we have chosen. It is astonishing where weeks, months and years of purposeful progress will take us and just how rewarding the view is on the way. It beats the road-to-nowhere existence every time.

Space Inspiration

What better inspiration for our new journey than an expedition into space.

In the summer of 1977, NASA launched Voyager 1 and Voyager 2 from the Kennedy Space Center at Cape Canaveral in Florida on what, because of US Federal spending cuts at the time, was originally billed as a relatively modest two-planet mission featuring spacecraft that were designed to last five years.

Rather than rely on just the finite supply of nuclear power on board these twin probes, NASA decided to use the gravity of the moons and planets on the spacecraft's journey as a 'gravitational slingshot' to propel and redirect them around our solar system.

As a result, this dual mission, which is still under way, is now expected to last well into the 2020s, with Voyager 1 having already entered interstellar space, and Voyager 2 heading for the same destination. All of this from an expedition that should, in theory, have ended back in the 1980s.

Just as those apparently expendable probes, built on a budget, have rewritten the history of modern space exploration, we too are free to reach for the stars and have the courage to dream.

The real inspiration of Voyagers 1 and 2 is the power they have received *during and from* their journey. Their expedition made them, and is still making them, more than anything they ever were at the start.

Each planet and moon they have visited has given them more energy and renewed direction. In the same way, every destination on our financial journey will give us a sense of reward, momentum and energy that we had never previously thought possible—one that will, in turn, point us to our next goal.

Destinations

Before any worthwhile journey, comes a plan—our chance to pick our destinations; the goals we will achieve on the way.

These are more than just stopping-off points—they are milestones, each one providing us with a source of reward and inspiration that will lead us to even greater achievements. And while our journey has to start in the present, it does not need to be defined *by* the present. Although we need to accept where we are now, we are encouraged to indulge our passions and to envisage the future that we will be creating.

So what would we like our first, and subsequent, destinations to be? What places are we going to actively visit on our financial journey? Now is the time to decide. Now is the time to take the first of our 12 steps on the roadmap to financial success.

Paying our bills on time for the next three months?

Paying off our credit card, which has started to take on a life of its own?

Buying a home?

Investing in, and starting, our own business?

Having enough money to travel the world and experience different languages and cultures?

Being able to afford to spend more time with our children before their 936 weeks of childhood are snatched away from us?

Maybe it is none of these, maybe one, and maybe several—one goal at a time, with each goal opening the door to the next.

Picking our destinations is at once exciting and intimidating. Breaking away from our familiar, predictable existence and choosing the exit road straight out of our comfort zone is never something that comes naturally.

But we can take strength from the knowledge that the directions given within this book point to a tried, tested and proven path. Unlike those fabled maritime expeditions of old, the ultimate forerunners of the Voyager project, we know that there is no danger of falling off the edge of the earth. There is no mission-critical scenario from which we cannot recover. There is no reason not to embark on the adventure. Which, in itself, is a compelling reason to do so.

Staging Posts

When we open our mind to a journey, we tend to undertake a mental leap straight to the final destination, but the staging posts that lead up to this point are just as important.

Nowhere is this disconnect in our society, between starting point and journey's end, more evident than in the world of personal finance. We are encouraged to plan for our retirement and make provision for our death, irrespective of our ability to manage our everyday life in the form of our day-to-day finances. It is the equivalent of trying to handle a powerful motorcycle, without ever having learned to ride a bike.

The information contained within these pages creates a new context—one which encourages us to learn and take control.

In the same way that a person's first step is a rite of passage that defines the end of babyhood, the first achievement on our financial journey is what I term 'unspectacularly spectacular'.

Just like the foundations of a tall building, which can be months in the making. At a superficial level, nothing seems to be happening when, in fact, nothing could be further from the truth. A basis is being put in place that, although unassuming, will support the massive structure that is to follow.

Similarly, those seemingly unremarkable three months of punctual repayments have the power to set the scene for a new financial future; an odyssey that is a departure from all we have ever known.

Let the journey begin!

Step 2:

The Starting Point of Our Journey

Our Current Financial Situation

There is nothing more exciting than the prospect of setting off on a journey. Especially to a destination we are longing to visit. Having defined the destination, therefore, we are feeling correspondingly motivated.

The buzz of the journey is such that it even extends to its preparation. Something that, in turn, only serves to heighten our sense of anticipation.

At the beginning of this sequence of events was our choice of destination, the importance of which is self-evident. What is not so obvious, however, is the second step on the roadmap to financial success: deciding where the journey starts. That is to say, determining where we are right now.

This is reminiscent of the old joke in which, when someone asks us for directions to a particular place, we reply that it would be best not to start from here. Like any good joke, this answer is both true and ludicrous in equal measure.

The same applies to our current location. Because our starting-point is less than ideal we have, if we wish, a ready-made excuse not to start at all. In truth, though, this unsatisfactory place is just the reason that we *should* be trying to bring about change.

It is also important to accept our true location, rather than to fool ourselves that things are actually better than they are. By believing that we are closer to the destination than we really are, we will underestimate the road in front of us, become disappointed and be more likely to abandon the journey as a result.

In the event, for example, that we have built up high levels of high-interest debt over several years, we should not expect to become debt-free in a matter of days, weeks or even months. Indeed, the emphasis should be on changing our behaviour, rather than reducing debt. A focus on the former is, over time, likely to be the most effective means of achieving the latter.

And if we are planning to undertake the journey with a partner, it is important that we are both cognisant of our current whereabouts. When two people are pulling in opposite directions, no journey will ever get started. With those same people pulling together, though, we double our chances of success. By 'sharing the drive', we take the hard yards out of the miles ahead.

Financial Disorientation

In aviation, spatial disorientation accounts for much avoidable loss of life, especially among pilots of small planes. Someone who succumbs to this phenomenon, defined by Wikipedia as "…a condition in which an aircraft pilot's perception of direction does not agree with reality", enters an altered state of existence.

In these circumstances, the stress of a deteriorating situation can serve to reinforce a pilot's mistaken perception of where they find themselves. This state of delusion can be so strong that it has the power to defy all logic. Not even a battery of instrument readings disproving the pilot's assumption about the aircraft's location can challenge this tunnel vision. Once in place, this unshakeable mindset represents one of the most serious risks to a pilot's survival.

Before this phenomenon was identified, pilots were given no preventative training and had no way of recognising if they were in the grip of such a threat. Nowadays, though, it is a fundamental component of any aviator's education. Budding pilots are made thoroughly familiar with spatial disorientation—its existence, its tell-tale signs and its prevention.

'Financial disorientation' can represent just as potent a threat to our economic survival. A state of delusion so compelling that it prevents us from escaping the imminent danger represented by the condition of our finances.

The most effective antidote to spatial disorientation is for a pilot to trust in and follow their instruments, rather than their gut feeling.

We, too, need to heed the tangible indicators of our financial situation, be it our deteriorating account balance, our mounting debts or the escalating demands from our creditors.

We also need to listen to advice that is dispensed from any trusted source. If our financial equivalent of the control tower were to tell us that we are on a disastrous heading and need to change direction fast, we would be well advised to pay careful attention.

Getting Real

Assuming that we *are* open to reality and wish to address our financial challenges, it is important to get real without getting critical. We are all gifted in the art of kicking ourselves when we are down. But such behaviour only heaps pain on pain and prevents us from moving forward.

By dispassionately assessing our current circumstances, including how they came about, we give ourselves the best chance of never repeating the mistakes of the past and, moreover, of starting on the path that will lead us to our destination.

The same ground rules apply to anyone external who might be helping us along the way. The proof that they are the right person at the right time in our life is not the letters after their name or their years of financial experience, but the fact that they refrain from judgement or criticism and encourage, rather than discourage.

Unintentional discouragement is an all-too-common by-product of the personal finance industry as a whole. In marketing to the masses, large portions of the population are placed into very large boxes according to where they *should* be at any given time in their lives. Assumptions which do nothing to help the many people whose finances fall outside of such a model of established norms.

What really matters is that, at some point in our life, we learn from our mistakes and, as a result, start to move in the right direction. It is this very movement towards something better—as opposed to our static position on someone else's theoretical scale—that is the ultimate indicator of our success.

Our Whereabouts

So what *are* the coordinates of our current location? And how can we make this unenviable place into a life-changing landmark—the beginning of something new?

Maybe we are trapped in a pattern of wasteful behaviour that is depriving us of our financial future.

It might be that our position can be defined by a sinister 'credit creep', which has been almost invisibly supplementing our earnings over the past few years.

Perhaps bills and debts soak up so much of our time and energy that they rob us of the feeling of aliveness that we once had.

Often, we find ourselves struggling to cope with the consequences of a financial commitment we made in the past—frequently, involving the purchase of a shiny new car—a decision that would now play out very differently as part of our newfound financial enlightenment.

Or, possibly, we fought with all of our might to keep our head above the financial waterline. But the day our finances went into the red was the day we threw in the proverbial towel and, by default, chose to be powerless over our financial fate.

Any one of these circumstances can be the financial equivalent of a bad case of sunburn. Just as the gentlest touch to the exposed area of skin can cause untold pain so, when we are suffering financial stress, even the smallest of bills can trigger major anguish.

The discomfort we feel is synonymous with a lack of control and is often associated with financial fear. Like the child who is scared of the dark, it can seem easier to hide under the covers and choose to live our life in financial gloom, rather than face up to that fear.

In this situation, we might even have come to agree with the widely accepted maxim that money is at the root of all evil. When, in reality, money itself is simply a medium, incapable of demonstrating goodness, badness or anything in between. Perhaps this old adage conveniently justified our decision to have as little to do with money as possible. In which case, as a result, money doubtless reciprocated by staying well away from us.

Whatever the reason for the lack of financial control that characterises the place we currently find ourselves in, it is never too late to reclaim the authority over our destiny that is our birthright. As part of this process, the very acknowledgement of our own particular challenges is a crucial enabler of our impending journey.

As long as this acceptance of where we are at is full and frank, it can mark the beginning of an incredibly productive, long-term engagement with our finances and the start of a new journey. One on which we connect with money, attract it back into our world, and swap our financial dead-end with an inestimable life-long opportunity.

Step 3:

Our Means of Transport

The Power of a Budget

When Adelir Antônio de Carli, a Catholic priest, strapped himself into a chair attached to helium party balloons, on Sunday April 20, 2008, and floated six kilometres skywards, it was one heck of a farewell to the mere mortals down below. Not that it was ever intended to be, though.

His ascension into heaven was originally meant to raise money for a good cause here on Earth. That same day, however, this flight of fancy morphed into a trip of terror, as the Brazilian pastor found himself, effectively, with a one-way ticket to meet his boss.

Suspended from 1,000 brightly-coloured balloons, Padre Baloneiro, as he was known to his flock, was at the mercy of the winds, which defied God's plan and blew him out over the Atlantic Ocean.

He did have a mobile phone with him, but it appeared the battery had not been fully charged. And he also had a GPS device, but it transpired that he had never bothered to learn how to use it. As a result, not even a miracle could save him. When rescuers searched in vain for the multi-coloured heavenly object, Father Baloneiro's fate—in the form of a premature rendezvous with his maker—was well and truly sealed.

Party balloons, it is safe to conclude, are not a recommended form of transport. Their absolute lack of direction and total reliance on external forces that are beyond our (or, apparently, even any supernatural) control regarding the path they assume, make for a completely arbitrary journey.

Strange though it may seem, though, they are a more common form of carriage than one might imagine. Our courageous cleric had, for example, already ascended to the heavens and lived to tell the tale some three months previously, when his then 600 balloons took him five kilometres high and 25 kilometres in distance over a period of four hours.

Arbitrary journeys, then, can deliver us to perfect places, just as easily as they can take us to problematic ones. And that is their drawback; their complete absence of certainty or predictability. This game of chance is what we need to put an end to if we are to take complete control over our own financial journey and its destination. In order to do this, we need to adopt a means of financial transport, in the form of a budget, with the promise of certainty instead. Welcome to step three on our roadmap to financial success.

Definition of a Budget

At this point, it is worth defining exactly what I mean by a budget, as it can signify different things to different people.

I am referring to a single, unified system, such as a customised spreadsheet or purpose-built software, which embraces the whole of our personal finances.

Which tracks all revenue, all spending and, ultimately, all cash flow, in the form of today's account balance and a forecast of our account balance on any given day in the future.

Which reports and predicts reality, shows us the trajectory of our finances, and enables us to make informed choices by running a whole range of hypothetical scenarios.

Which is a repository of information, a crystal ball and a trusted advisor all in one.

Once we have experienced the financial surefootedness that comes from living by a budget, we never want to go back. The party-balloon lifestyle of unpredictability, fun though it is, never holds the same appeal again.

I have come across people who tell me that their budget involves noting down what they spend. This might be a useful financial exercise, but it does not, in itself, constitute a budget. To record spending in isolation is reactive and backward-looking, whereas a budget is about taking control and looking to the future. The habit of logging outgoings is to a fully-fledged budget what Fred Flintstone's foot-powered automobile is to a muscle car. One will get us as far as the Bedrock Drive-In; the other will leave the town of Bedrock for dust.

Living within our Means

A budget ensures that we live within our means. This seemingly-unassuming accomplishment is the achievement which enables everything that then follows.

The phrase 'to live within one's means' trips off the tongue in a way that belies the challenge conveyed by the words. The main problem is to know just what those means are.

In the 19th century, it was pretty easy to work them out. That was when Charles Dickens penned his much-quoted recipe for happiness, which went something like, 'Annual income twenty pounds, annual expenditure nineteen pounds, result happiness.

Annual income twenty pounds, annual expenditure twenty pounds and six, result misery.'

Back then, income was paid in cash, as was expenditure. The consumer society was still in its infancy, and so most people lead economically unsophisticated lives. Our modern financial sophistication can sometimes feel more like unnecessary complication.

The plethora of modern service providers that support any one life and the corresponding array of non-cash payment methods make it easy to lose track of much of our financial existence. Modern personal finances would have blown the minds of Dickens and his contemporaries. Little wonder, then, that most inhabitants of the 21st century are not even close to being on top of it all.

The level of complexity of the modern world means that we need to promote ourselves by becoming the self-appointed CEO of our own life if we are to move ahead on our journey. And, just as a slick financial operation is the real power behind any successful CEO, a well-run budget is what gives us a business-like authority over our own endeavours. Providing us with the type information about our means, and how to live and thrive within them, that Dickens and his cronies could take for granted. Back in the 19th century, they did not need to impose a system to gain control of their finances, but we certainly do.

Financial Overview

A budget also gives us an indispensable overview of our financial circumstances. We have all heard accounts of people who have become disorientated in a forest and quickly lost their way. What should have been a relatively simple task—that of re-emerging from the vegetation—quickly became very complicated, all because of a few misguided moves. The nearest road in these situations is often tantalisingly close, yet frustratingly elusive.

If the protagonist of the story could somehow have been given a bird's-eye view of their terrain, they would, no doubt, have quickly found a way out of their inhospitable surroundings.

The financial forest which we sometimes get lost in means that one wrong move compounds the next, and so on, to often devastating effect. We then become engrossed in our struggle for monetary survival and so trapped in the 'money myopia' of a payday-to-payday perspective that we fail to view our situation from another standpoint.

When we are handed a map of the territory, though, seeing our financial conditions from the big-picture viewpoint of a budget is, invariably, a revelation.

The landscape suddenly appears so much less threatening. It is as if, seen from above, we are given a superhuman power over our environment. And even if that all-important road back to financial civilisation is some distance away, at least it is visible and, therefore, reachable.

This control over our financial situation and the associated sense of hope is what a budget gives us. Information is power, and it is the very information contained in the overview of our budget, our financial map, that empowers us.

It is the very opposite of the powerlessness we experience when we have reached a financial dead-end and can no longer pay our bills. When creditors, debt collectors and lawyers impose their control over us. When our own will counts for nothing and is utterly disregarded.

Living by a Budget

The path, if there were one, which takes us to such an objectionable place, would probably be labelled 'least resistance'. It is the one we default to when we do not have a plan.

Drawing up and living by a budget involves us following a completely different route to this well-trodden, yet remarkably-unfulfilling, path. It is about taking responsibility for where we are now and learning from it, so that we can steer ourselves towards a new future.

A budget is not a magic cure. To quote Maria in the The Sound of Music, "Nothing comes from nothing, nothing ever could." It requires time and effort. It is a proactive, goal-orientated approach to our financial existence, which is characterised by short-term pain and long-term gains.

Because a budget is anything other than 'more of the same', these long-term gains include the elimination of waste from our finances, so that it can be recycled into cash. This day-to-day waste comes in many forms.

Failing to pay bills on time might be leading to regular late-payment fees. If one of these unpaid bills was our statutory annual vehicle fee, this pattern of behaviour might also have landed us with a hefty fine.

Less obviously, but no less important, late payments have the power to tarnish our repayment history and credit record which, of course, is just the beginning. This threatens our innate freedom to make choices in the management of our finances. This lack of financial freedom puts us at a significant and ongoing disadvantage. It can, for example, cut off our access to credit or mean that we are forced to pay more for any loan that we do qualify for.

Uncontrolled day-to-day spending is less visible than attention-grabbing fees and interest but, nonetheless, accounts for a huge amount of unnecessary outgoings.

The good news, though, is that all of this waste represents a high potential upside. By eradicating these habits, a budget can markedly increase our disposable income. It is as if we had increased our earnings without having to work any harder. And while most people focus on earning interest on their savings, it is my experience that cutting waste out of their budget can earn them a lot more.

This 'efficiency dividend', when coupled with the predictability of a well-run budget, means that we can quickly start to forecast which of our goals we will be able to achieve and when; making living by a personal budget the next best thing to being a clairvoyant.

On one level, therefore, living according to a budget is a no-brainer. On another, however, it is not yet mainstream financial behaviour in our society.

One reason for this might be the common misconception that a budget is all about frugality when, ultimately, it is actually about enrichment.

The only way that anything in life can have value is if it is finite; limited in some way. If gold literally paved the streets, it would have the same value as earth or dirt. And it is the finite nature of money that, once respected as such, will power our life's journey to infinite abundance.

If we treat money as limitless by living life on credit, for example, money can, and will, have no value to us. The only way to have money obey our wishes is to value it. And that means treating it as the finite resource it really is.

And if this idea seems too abstract, it is worth watching the documentary *Born Rich* by Jamie Johnson, the then 21-year-old heir to the Johnson & Johnson fortune. This film about his social clique, comprised of the sons and daughters of other billionaires—the Bloombergs, the Trumps and the Vanderbilts—demonstrates just how easy it is for money to lose its value when it is in virtually unlimited supply. After making the movie, he discovered that "…what you inherit may not be as valuable as what you earn." Confirming the paradox that a limited stream of money has more real value than an infinite amount.

Having our budget power us on our life's journey, therefore, has nothing to do with being rich or poor. Money doesn't equal abundance, but—by valuing it and respecting the role it plays as a means to an end in our life—it certainly has the power to create it.

Managing the Micro

Another reason, I believe, why budgeting is not standard behaviour for us is that a budget is about micro-managing our finances—something that, let's be honest, is not seen as desirable. It is just not fashionable, probably because it is perceived as being time consuming.

Micro-management is, in turn, about having complete control. And being in control, too, is not a good look—synonymous, as it is, with being a 'control freak'.

I see these labels, however, as being meaningless fads. I would argue that we should only move to the 'macro' once we have mastered the micro. That we are only ready to make, and exploit in full, the big financial calls in our life once micro-managing our money becomes second nature to us; once we are in total control of our day-to-day finances.

Anything that we do every day becomes—by definition—easy and, therefore, not time consuming. I'm sure that even rocket science becomes straightforward if we do it every day. And micro-managing our finances is no exception. This level of control and competency provides the basis for all of our future financial success.

The accepted thing to do to give direction to our finances, though, is to go to an accountant, a bank or financial planner. And while each of these has their own undoubted area of expertise, teaching us the day-to-day management of our finances is not one of them.

A financial planner, for example, might provide us with a budgeting spreadsheet but, if we do not complete it, it is of little consequence, as financial micro-management is not what they are about.

Similarly, having a vision-wall in our home is all well and good, but it is like a racing car without an engine if there is no day-to-day plan in place to ensure that the dreams on the wall become reality. 'Joining the dots' between the here and now and our aspirations is the real strength of any good budget.

Fact-Based Decision-Making

Living without a budget tends to mean that we use our energy to focus on the past tense. That we are regularly extinguishing the 'spot fires' of recent financial decisions, which can appear without warning in the here and now.

Servicing the sky-high balance of our low-rate credit card, for example. Trying to meet the loan repayments on the shiny new car that seemed like such a good idea when we were in the showroom. Or paying off last year's dream holiday that has since become a financial nightmare.

At best, these fires are a constant distraction from the present. At worst, they merge into one and engulf our financial world.

Living by a budget means leading an information-rich existence, which allows us to make purchasing decisions based on hard facts, as opposed to vacuous impulses. This does not mean that we can never again opt to buy a shiny new car or a dream holiday. It just means that, when we do, it will be in a completely informed way, such that we can enjoy these acquisitions in full, without fear of any unexpected costs.

By freeing us from the 'Groundhog Day' scenario of a predictable dose of daily drama, we are finally able to look to the future and have our money take us on the journey which it is there to do.

Step 4:

Rebuilding Our Engine

Drawing up our Budget

There is a saying that the best time to plant a tree is 20 years ago, and the second best time is now. I, though, subscribe to the view that the best time to do so is actually now.

It is all very well planting a tree but, in order for it to flourish, the conditions have to be right. A tree that was planted long ago in poor soil would have withered or died since then.

Going through our share of pain—even two decades or more of it—to arrive at the realisation that something needs to change involves us dealing with our own metaphorical manure which, of course, makes for the most fertile of soils.

Thus, we create—thanks to the challenges we have been through and the life lessons they have taught us—a perfect environment for our delicate but beautiful sapling to grow and thrive.

These conditions, of pain, yearning for change and willingness to follow a new path, which have the power to give rise to huge progress, have to be earned. They are a mark of the emotional maturity that is the prerequisite for sustainable success in any significant new chapter of our life.

No-one (not even a rich-and-powerful parent) can gift this state to us. No detours or short-cuts will get us there. And it is not possible to outsource the experience that brings us to this point to anyone else.

Arriving at this moment is an achievement in itself.

Financial Motor

Having selected our destination, determined our starting point and opted for a fully-fledged budget as our transport, now is the time to look under the bonnet. To get to work on our financial engine, the mechanism that will power this mode of transport.

If our life is not progressing, the chances are that we have probably lost sight of what we should be expecting of our financial motor. To propel us from one destination to the next with renewed momentum at each milestone we pass; a radical shift in most people's thinking.

In order to make this expectation a reality, it is time to strip down what there is of our financial engine and build an impressive power plant, one part at a time. One that is fit to start and sustain us on the ambitious journey we have planned for ourselves.

This is the nitty-gritty of our budgeting journey. If you are intent on creating a budget, therefore, the remainder of this chapter is for you. If, however, you do not feel ready to 'roll up your sleeves' and put together your own financial system just yet, you might want to consider jumping to the next step now and coming back to this material at a later date.

Building a Budget

When embarking on step four of the roadmap to financial success, by building our budget and entering income and expenditure data into our chosen software, it is important to record, as precisely as possible, any seasonal fluctuations. If earnings vary according to the time of year, if electricity bills are high in winter and low in summer, and so on. Any such seasonal factors need to be reflected over a full year in order to make our budget comprehensive, as well as accurate. To do this, pay slips, bills, and so on, from the past 12 months are an invaluable resource.

In the case of any reoccurring transactions, the time dimension of these repeating payments is a crucial component. It is therefore important to accurately record when, and with what frequency, income and bills are due to be paid. If a payment is monthly, for instance, what date of the month is it due? If it is weekly, what day of the week?

The reason for this is twofold. Firstly, getting ahead on bills if our finances are in a fragile state is not a great idea. In the utilities department, for example, we should be paying what we owe by the due date. Pay too much and too early, and we rob ourselves of cash flow and run the risk of falling behind elsewhere.

Secondly, when we do accurately record the time element of all recurring transactions, the budget we create benefits from a hologram-like depth that the aspect of time gives it. And this, in turn, ensures an accurate cash flow forecast.

The importance of a budget in tracking and forecasting cash flow, in the form of our account balance, cannot be overstated. This function is, in fact, the very essence of a budget. Just as accounting, as a discipline, is ultimately about the calculation of profit to establish tax liability, budgeting is all about recording and predicting our account balance to ascertain that outgoings can be met. And, although it might sound very dry, this ability to, more or less, foretell the future imbues us with the kind of control over our financial affairs—and, therefore, our life—that is both empowering and addictive.

Spreadsheets that attempt to reflect revenue and expenditure without reference to cash flow fall short of being fully-blown budgets. And those that try to break this income-and-outgoings data up into artificial bite-size chunks, by calculating an average week, as opposed to our actual week, will never succeed in guiding us through the longer-term vagaries of real life.

Dividing monthly rent by about four, for example, in order to express it as part of that illusive standard week, does nothing to forecast all-important daily cash flow. Trying to reduce each week to an average week is akin to having a single wardrobe all year round for life in a temperate climate. One set of clothes to wear, regardless of sleet and snow or baking-hot sunshine. It just doesn't work.

Income

Generally speaking, net income is the logical place to start when inputting data to build our budget. In order to do this, we have to be sure to capture all income. Wages, bonuses, commissions, overtime earnings, tax returns, business income, welfare payments, child-support—all relevant revenue ingredients need to be thrown into this pot. These are the famous 'means' that we are required to live within. It feels good to quantify them, to finally nail them down.

Indeed, putting a number on things has almost become a modern human addiction. Nowhere was this better illustrated than in Douglas Adams' novel The Hitchhiker's Guide to the Galaxy, in which the supercomputer Deep Thought calculated that, "The answer to the ultimate question of life, the universe and everything is…42."

In Deep Thought's case this number was, apparently, the conclusion of 7½ million years of calculations. In our case, the quantification of our means marks the starting point in the creation of our budget—the number which defines the space that we now have to play in.

Outgoings

After inputting our means in the form of our income, we can now enter our outgoings in the form of debt repayments, rent, mobile phone costs and so on.

As well as such frequent payments, we also need to be sure not to neglect annual transactions, such as statutory vehicle fees or insurance premiums. Not to mention other less-frequent items, such as children's school-related costs—extra-curricular activities, excursions and the like.

Other outgoings might include ad-hoc medical expenses. Where these are continuing, but not regular or predictable, they do not fit easily into a budgetary system. My recommendation would be to come up with an average monthly amount and to allocate this sum as a regular expense in the budget—due, for example, at the beginning of each month. This amount could be withdrawn as cash and kept separate from any other funds, so that it is used only for its intended purpose.

When it comes to debt repayments, a baseline assumption of our budgetary system needs to be the ability to meet our minimum repayments. In the case of a credit card, for example, if the budget does not, at this stage, allow any principal (debt) to be paid off, it should at least allow for the minimum applicable monthly repayments to be made.

These might not sound like impressive expectations, but it all comes back to the 'unspectacularly spectacular' nature of our budget. An ongoing solvent budget and minimum credit repayments probably appear unspectacular when compared to our dreams. These achievements might well, though, be spectacular when compared to our recent financial past.

As long, of course, as we are truthful with ourselves about what that recent past entailed and what, if anything, it was leading to. Imagine, for example, that we have racked up high-interest debt over a number of years. Because we have become so used to this debt, we probably do not realise that its very existence denotes that we have been living beyond our means. If we are oblivious to this fact, we are unlikely to be motivated by the prospect of a break-even budget that does not involve taking on any new debt. If, however, we are fully aware of the downward trajectory of our financial past, we are likely to embrace a plan that plots a course towards a sustainable financial future.

At this early stage, the name of the game is to build a budget that represents an improved, more-disciplined version of our current existence, as opposed to reflecting our ideal life. Getting this functioning financial engine on the road is the aim. It is about pragmatism over perfectionism.

The perfecting of the budget is what can follow at a later stage, which usually begins with a growth in savings or a higher underlying account balance. These extra funds then present us with options. The chance, for example, to increase our regular debt repayments or to pay down some of the principal in chunks.

Economics talks about the 'marginal benefit' of doing something. This is the additional satisfaction which is derived from acquiring an extra unit of a commodity or service that we already have. The first drink we consume on a hot day is the one which delivers the most pleasure—that first beverage being the equivalent of our initial, functioning budget. Similar to the law of diminishing returns, the additional pleasure derived from each subsequent drink then becomes less and less.

In the same way, perfecting our budget—increasing the power of our existing financial engine—is what we do over time to gain a marginal benefit. But it is the very fact of having a budget, no matter how modest its initial achievements, that is of greatest value to us.

That is why we should regard the financial engine which we are now building as being scalable, with power being able to be increased, as required. Not to mention the momentum that will naturally accrue on our journey, as if to reward us for our ongoing perseverance.

Management of Outgoings

In the case of reoccurring outgoings, I recommend subdividing these in our budget software. The first subcategory being for *ongoing identical payment amounts*.

These payments are likely to be preprogrammed in our internet banking. This 'fire-and-forget' way of paying these constant amounts, such as rent, is an effective labour-saving device in the operation of our budget.

The second subcategory is for *ongoing variable payment amounts*, such as utilities payments and minimum monthly credit card repayments.

It also includes annual payments, such as insurance premiums and statutory vehicle fees. Because these tend to increase year-on-year they, too, are variable amounts.

And it can include provision for vehicle servicing, be it quarterly, half-yearly, or annually. Such costs are very relevant to any budget but can be difficult to predict and, therefore, variable in nature.

I also suggest giving these *ongoing variable payment amounts* a different colour within our budget in order to reflect the fact that they are, effectively, 'pencilled-in' amounts.

To take a utility payment as an example: once the latest bill has been received and we have programmed this particular payment into our internet banking ahead of time, or this payment has been made by direct debit (whereby the provider of the service has debited our account), we then change the estimated amount shown in our budget to the actual amount for this transaction (assuming the two are different). And we also change the colour of this transaction back to the standard colour in our spreadsheet, to show that it is an actual payment, as opposed to an estimated amount.

This helps us to distinguish between estimated future amounts and actual transactions.

In order to arrive at the estimated future *ongoing variable payment amounts* as part of the process of building our budget, we should take an average of the most recent actual amounts.

Living Expenses

Having input all income and outgoings, we now get to find out what is left over for our living expenses, which include grocery shopping, petrol, coffees, take-away food and eating out.

The cost of smoking, too, is a form of living expenses. Where smoking is applicable, it is advisable, for two reasons, to list cigarettes as a separate living expense item in our budget. Firstly, smoking tends to be an expensive habit, and so it is important for any budget to accurately reflect this cost. Secondly, as a separate expense, attention is drawn to the amount being spent, which can act as an incentive to quit. Aside from the obvious health benefits of quitting, this then creates valuable extra cash flow.

The reason for inputting living expenses last of all is that they are more pliable than our income and other relatively-inflexible outgoings. If necessary, the amount allocated for living expenses can be reduced to help balance our budget. We should, though, be realistic about how much we require to live off week in and week out. When needs must, anyone can go without for a week or so, but this is not something we should be asking of ourselves on an ongoing basis. When systems fall down, most people give up on them. And one of the easiest ways for our financial system to fail is if we underestimate the amount we need for living expenses.

Being realistic about what we need to live off is easier said than done, with most people's estimate falling far short of reality. In order to 'bed this amount down', it is best to monitor what we spend over the first four weeks of our budget. By doing so, we get to work out an average weekly requirement, as opposed to basing our ongoing figure on a random given week.

Surplus Funds

Following this all-important allocation of living expenses, if we happen to find ourselves in the happy position of forecasting a surplus, there is a number of things that we might want to consider doing.

Firstly, to simply let this extra amount accrue for the first few months so that we establish a healthy account-balance buffer.

Secondly, we could earmark surplus funds for foreseeable annual costs, such as Christmas and birthdays. This is a practice that I can only encourage. My suggestion would be to apportion a set amount in our budget that we could withdraw two weeks prior to the birthday of each immediate family member, and a larger amount four weeks before Christmas, to cover all associated costs, including present-buying. If it sounds good in theory, it feels even better in practice. As the event in question draws near and we find ourselves with the cash we need, it is both a relief and a pleasure to be able to celebrate in the knowledge that there will be no financial hangover.

Thirdly, we could, at this early stage, plan to set money aside to enable our goals. This might involve paying off debt or saving up for a specific purpose or both. Our objective could be to save for something as simple as a weekend away (as holidays and trips away are not usually a default inclusion in any budget, especially at the beginning) to something as ambitious as a deposit for a house.

We might also wish to use our budget to ascertain what goals are possible. How many months can we afford to go travelling for? How long can we live off one income if we decide to have a baby? When does our new business need to start paying us a wage?

The ability to simulate our financial goals, whatever they may be, is where our newly-created budget comes into its own. Once we have decided which scenarios we wish to pursue, we might choose to put money aside in order to make them happen. Probably the most practical way of doing this is to set up a regular deposit of funds into a separate interest-bearing account.

By extension, it is also feasible to have multiple such accounts, each one assigned to a different purpose. As long, of course, as this does not overcomplicate our finances. Numerous accounts and complicated banking structures tend to be synonymous with chaotic finances. Transparency and simplicity are the hallmarks of any well run budget.

Finally, we might want to use our forecast surplus to save for saving's sake. Indeed, the accumulation of savings can be a goal in itself. This does not, though, always need to involve a savings account. Paradoxically, a debt facility can present us with one of the best options for creating savings. Getting ahead on our mortgage repayments, for example, can be a great way to save as, if these extra funds are paid into the redraw facility of our home loan, they can, as the name suggests, be redrawn at a later date, if needed. And, by paying extra onto our home loan, the benefit we derive is at the loan's rate of interest, which is higher than the deposit rate.

In fact, if we get into the regular habit early on of paying extra off our home loan, the results we achieve—in terms of the interest repayments we save and the number of years we cut our home loan by—can be astonishing. This is because the majority of the interest costs are charged in the first few years of the loan, when the amount that is owed is at its highest.

And because getting ahead on our home loan, effectively, involves increasing our equity stake in what is hopefully an appreciating asset, this is likely to be the most productive method of saving money that we have.

Building up savings might also include for our children. If this is the case, and if we do not yet have any savings of our own, I recommend a modest children's savings plan to begin with. People tend to feel guilty if they do not put a reasonable amount aside for their children. As parents, though, the accumulation of our own savings as a financial buffer for the whole family should have priority.

As a rule, it is important to address our own financial problems before thinking about helping others. When donating to charity, we need to ensure that we are far from needing charity ourselves. That way, once we do decide to give to others as part of our budget, we will prove our worth as a reliable financial donor many times over.

When it comes to savings, some financial pundits have hard-and-fast expectations as to what needs to be achieved. A given percentage of our annual income sitting in an emergency fund, for example. The problem with this dogmatic approach is that it gives us the feeling that we are behind before we have even started. That we are running a deficit, just because we have not yet reached our savings target.

Rather than adhere to such financial doctrine, my emphasis is on learning to value, and gain control of, our money. The healthy habits which then ensue empower us to make our own decisions about what is appropriate for us, and our particular circumstances, in terms of saving, spending, and paying off debt.

Balancing the Budget

The process of creating a budget is an exercise in 'painting by numbers'. Each data entry adds to the canvas, on which a picture of our finances now begins to appear. Our previously hidden financial life now emerges as an information-rich tapestry, with each little detail giving the overall composition a remarkable clarity.

Once the creative process is complete, it is time to review our finished work. Just as the face of a familiar voice on the radio rarely turns out to be what we had envisioned, so the financial portrait that materialises is often not what we had expected.

Sometimes, the surprise will be a pleasant one, and our forecast bank account balance will be positive for the next 365 days and trending upwards over the long term (both signs of a healthy budget). And sometimes, not so pleasant, with a negative forecast, which is then set to deteriorate even further.

The remedy for such a confronting scenario might be to cut outgoings or increase income or both. When no amount of tweaking income and expenditure will allow our financial engine to fire, though, it could be that our finances are structurally unsound, and that our outgoings, including any loan repayment commitments, are far in excess of anything we could ever afford in our current situation.

In such circumstances, we might have to contemplate drastic measures in order to be able to live within our means. This could involve downsizing, getting out of property (if we are home owners) or opting for a change of career. And, although at the time, being faced with the stark reality of our financial condition is demoralising, the budget we have drawn up can be instrumental in guiding us down the right path. In this context, calculating our annual overspend often empowers us to take the kind of bold action that is called for.

Sometimes, smoothing out future cash flow is the key to the viability of a new budget. This might be accomplished by arranging with service providers to pay set weekly amounts, as opposed to making payments that are both less frequent and less predictable. Whether such arrangements stay in place long after the budget has 'taken off', or whether they are dismantled once they have achieved their aim, is very much a matter of personal preference.

Occasionally, when a new budget cannot be made to balance, credit can provide the solution. I know that many people who wish to draw up and live by a budget have had their fingers burnt with credit in the past—be it a personal loan, a car loan or a credit card. This does not, however, mean that all credit is bad. Responsible credit, as part of a structured, disciplined budget, is not comparable to the phenomenon of an almost imperceptible dependence on ever-increasing amounts of debt to fund lifestyle.

Everyone's circumstances are, of course, different and, as such, it is always best to seek personal advice in the case of any credit application. A typical scenario in which credit might make the difference between the success and failure of a new budget, though, is when our cash flow forecast, whilst initially going into the red, then follows a positive trajectory, which sees our account balance going into the black (including when the future repayments for the new credit facility we are currently contemplating are factored in).

It may be, for example, that this initially-negative cash flow forecast is caused by various arrears which are due right now. Each set of arrears might, in itself, not be dramatic. Taken together, however, they may have the power to bring us down, in the same way that an apparent mountain of a buffalo can be brought to its knees by a pack of hyenas. In such circumstances, a timely injection of credit could rescue our current cash flow and, by extension, the future of our finances.

Likewise, where we have significant credit card debt, it might be worth applying to take advantage of a low- or zero-interest-rate balance transfer offer (in which our current balance gets transferred to the new card, subject to the approval of our application and the conditions of any particular offer). If possible, our budget would allow for debt to be paid down more quickly during the low- or no-interest period. Again, such a move is far more likely to be effective in the context of a disciplined budget than if it is 'just another credit application'.

As part of this discipline, it is generally best to avoid making purchases using our new balance transfer credit card during the period of the special-interest-rate offer. The reason for this is twofold. Firstly, purchases tend to attract a higher interest rate than balance transfers.

Secondly, most credit card providers employ a 'negative payment hierarchy'. This ensures that any credit card repayments are prioritised to pay off the lower-interest-rate items in full, in the form of the balance transfer debt, before beginning to pay off the higher-interest-rate items, such as purchases. By gradually paying off the balance transfer amount over the period of the offer, therefore, any purchases we have made using the card are left to accrue interest during that time. Giving rise to a potentially unwelcome surprise in months to come.

Once we have achieved a balanced budget forecast it is time to pick a 'go-live' date. Maybe today, maybe tomorrow, or maybe our next payday. Before our chosen date, we should program in all of the regular, automated payments on internet banking that will be made as part of our budget. Such attention to detail will help ensure a seamless start.

Stress-Testing

During the Global Financial Crisis, there was a lot of media coverage about the need for banks to 'stress-test' their finances. And whilst this activity might appear to be the preserve of sophisticated financial institutions, the good news is that we are now in a position to do the same. Just like the simulation of our financial goals, our newly-created money management system enables us to anticipate any potentially-relevant stressful financial scenarios, such as being made redundant.

Because such circumstances can seem bleak, it is easy to overlook any related silver lining in the form, for instance, of reduced outgoings. Take the example of a parent losing their job. For a given time at least, public transport and childcare costs might fall away. Living expenses can probably be reduced, as can any debt repayments in excess of the minimum due amounts. Some form of welfare income might also become applicable.

If it transpires that we then experience this situation for real, it is as if we have been there already. Living by this budget, to use the military jargon, allows us to 'train hard' in our planning and 'fight easy' in the day-to-day execution of our finances. Empowering us to navigate our future like never before.

Step 5:

Hitting the Road

Starting to Live by a Budget

After all the preparation, it is time to move to the fifth step on our roadmap to financial success by hitting the road and getting our budget started.

When we buy a new car, we can't wait to get in and drive it. The same holds true of our new budget. Having invested the time and effort to put it together, we are now itching to use it.

And just as a new car quickly becomes an indispensable part of our day-to-day life, our budget now does the same. Whereas before, we probably didn't quite know what our finances were doing at any given time, we now start to be on top of them every day. Verifying that each transaction in our budget comes to fruition, ensuring the day's account balance is as per our forecast and looking at what the future holds.

This daily contact we now have with our finances is the beginning of a whole new relationship with them and a vital part of taking control of our money.

Checking in with our finances every day can sound daunting and time-consuming. In a matter of weeks, though, a well-run, systemised budget takes on a momentum of its own. Paradoxically, therefore, this daily routine actually frees up our time by allowing us to assume a kind of supervisory role. A refreshing and liberating development, especially if we are more used to the position of financial fire fighter.

New Reality

If our money was a mess before we started a budget, the chances are that, for quite some time, we had been 'living on a prayer', to quote Bon Jovi. Because our finances lacked a system, on some level, we probably fooled ourselves into thinking that we could spend whatever we wanted and achieve whatever we wished without any plan. By extension, once we transition to a budget, it can feel as if we have much less money than before. This is usually because we used to live under the illusion of unlimited financial resources. As part of which, our finances might well have been hooked up to a 'credit drip', which was almost invisibly supplementing our income.

Often, therefore, it is sobering to see—as part of a budget—the cold, hard reality of what is achievable in the short term. Especially when that short term might involve addressing legacy financial problems before we can start to move ahead.

A plane shows us how we can use an apparent obstacle to our advantage. Because it is the speed of a plane's wings through the air that generates lift, by flying *into* the wind, the plane moves through the air quicker than its wheels are able to propel it along the ground, thereby producing more lift. By utilising the headwind to its benefit, therefore, the speed of the plane's take-off is no longer restricted by the output of its engine.

By starting to face up to the obstacles in our way, including the limited nature of our financial resources, and embracing the challenges in our budget, we can rise above where we currently are, and keep on rising. These very obstacles have the power to make us stronger; to make us even more than we are right now.

Transparency and Connectedness

Embarking on this new course and living by a budget means living our life with consequences. And while consequences tend to be synonymous with costs and penalties, they are just as much about results and rewards. To live life without a financial system is to deny ourselves a sense of reward and achievement when we have earned it.

Living with consequences means that everything is connected. For every action there is an outcome.

In the practice of reflexology, each part of the foot has a seemingly invisible link to a different area of the body. Pressure applied to a specific area of the foot provokes a reaction elsewhere.

So it is with a budget. Each financial action gives rise to an outcome somewhere else in our life. And just as reflexology can predict the outcome of a given stimulus to the foot, so a budget forecasts the result of a given financial transaction.

The advantage of this transparency and connectedness is that the future consequences of today's actions are already apparent to us in the present. As a result, there are no more nasty surprises. No more future 'tense' and no more present 'tense', as we become aware of the holistic outcome of every transaction we make.

This connectedness, which now characterises our financial life, also means we can be confident that what we sow today, we will reap tomorrow. This, in turn, motivates us to proactively manage our finances in the present in order to build up tangible surpluses in the future.

Productive Practices

One of the easiest and most productive practices we can adopt in the context of our new budget is, where possible, to forego the immediate benefit of any improvement to our finances.

This may be in the form of a one-off cash injection. We might decide to have our credit card rewards points paid out as cash, for example. And, instead of blowing the proceeds, we could choose to save some or all of these funds instead. Prior to living by a budget, there would have been little or no incentive to do this, as the money would probably have disappeared sooner or later, anyway. In the context of a budget, though, this financial boost remains a highly visible entry on our personal 'balance sheet' and, as such, gives us an ongoing, tangible sense of reward for our decision to save it, rather than spend it.

In our newly connected, rewarding budget environment, what better thing to do than to engineer a financial gift that just keeps on giving. A good time to do this is if we are in line for a pay rise any time soon. Rather than 'take the money', we could continue to live off the same amount, deposit the extra into a savings account and watch it build into something more substantial with every payday that comes around.

Another such example could involve a drop in interest rates on a variable-interest credit facility, such as a home or personal loan. Rather than reduce our repayments in line with the drop, we might carry on repaying at the current level, and look on with satisfaction as our debt reduces at a faster rate.

Healthy Habits

Because money is such an important medium in our life, it tends to be an accurate barometer of our general patterns of behaviour. If we are punctual payers, it is likely that we are punctual by nature. If we practise healthy financial habits, the chances are that we are healthy eaters too, and so on.

When transitioning from no financial system to one that is ultimately good for us, we might well find ourselves switching from regular consumption of takeaways, crisps and soft drinks to a more healthy diet. Once we do, we soon realise that the only thing that was cheap about junk food were the ingredients, as we quickly start to see our savings accumulate.

As part of this more wholesome lifestyle, if we manage to cut down on—or cut out—cigarettes, the result can be akin to an ongoing windfall. And because our budget operates as much in the future as it does in the present, the gains that are yet to accrue can be nothing short of spectacular.

The rewards of a budget, in the form of the savings that can be made, act as a powerful incentive to be constantly on the look-out for new opportunities to save and, thereby, become tangibly better off.

Where lunch has been at the heart of our fast-food lifestyle, our midday meal might provide one such opportunity—as well as giving us a chance to lessen our midriff in the process. If we work full time and buy lunch every day, the savings we make in one day by packing our lunch multiplied by approximately 250 give us an idea of what we can achieve in a year. They say there's no such thing as a free lunch, but a packed one certainly comes pretty close.

The daily latte represents more low-hanging fruit or, should I say, beans. Money that is being poured away every day. Hot coffee that can be transformed into cold cash as part of our budget.

Caffeine can be every bit as addictive as nicotine. And, as with cigarettes, it is often the associated ritual that is powerfully compulsive. Only once we multiply the cost of heading to the café each day by 250, can we ask ourselves whether this routine is really giving us value for money year in and year out.

By clubbing together and buying a coffee machine at work, we would be helping our colleagues to 'save big' too. And by purchasing a machine for home as well, we can save even more and bring out our budding barista all at the same time. Everyone's a winner—except, of course, the local café. There is no reason, though, to not go there again. It is just that, when we do, it is seen as a treat. Proving, once again, that less is more, since we attach greater value to a restricted supply of a given commodity.

Coffee, lunch and cigarettes are daily occurrences. Some activities, such as grocery shopping, should be weekly, but have a habit of becoming daily, making them unnecessarily expensive.

A weekly shop tends to be far more economical than a daily 'raid' on the local store. Such sporadic incursions into supermarket territory (usually a male phenomenon, it has to be said) lack the strategy and coordination that is the hallmark of any effective military campaign.

By planning ahead and taking on seven days of supplies at any one time, the troops back at base will be kept happy, as basic provisions no longer keep running out. This system tends to work well if we purchase food with the next seven days of meals in mind, as opposed to just buying snacks. Thus, the phenomenon of the 'hungry belly' that returns, after an impulsive evening sortie, with more plunder than anyone knows what to do with, quickly becomes a thing of the past.

Indeed, it is a mathematical truism that Hunger + Food Shopping = Unnecessary Expense. As such, it is advisable to carry out these new regular weekly excursions on a full stomach, so that the rumblings from below are no longer allowed to take command. And if any young recruits are in tow, failing to feed them before letting them loose on these supply-line reinforcement missions can turn out to be a costly mistake.

When shopping for a particular food product, 'no-brand' is a no-brainer. By always looking for the equivalent own-brand supermarket item, we end up saving a packet.

And let's not forget that low price points often mean low display points. Checking out the contents of the low-margin bottom shelf can prove highly beneficial to our bottom line.

The destination of these manoeuvres is also a critical factor in saving big, with low-cost assets being prioritised over more expensive targets. We 'discount the discounters' at our peril. It is astonishing just how much we can save by learning to love our local low-price retailer and then topping up our rations, including the odd luxuries, at the more expensive 'full-choice' outlets. This procedure helps to ensure operational success every single week.

If an army marches on its belly, so does a budget. Grocery shopping, lunches, coffee and cigarettes can account for a significant part of our overall spend, making the 'dollar dividend' of getting this part of our budget right correspondingly important. Our systemised budget then translates the savings we make in these areas into lower costs this week, and for weeks, months and years into the future.

Step 6:

Driving the Drive

Spending Cash

If we do not have money, we probably do not have choices. The saying 'beggars cannot be choosers' shows how synonymous poverty is with a lack of choice.

The opposite, therefore, also holds true. Wealth and choice are compatible and mutually reinforcing. For better or for worse, the power of money cannot be underestimated.

If we wish to make money a force for the good in our life, we need to control it. And, just like breaking in a wild horse, this means training it by imposing a disciplined behavioural structure upon it. Only once this process is complete, once we are in total control, can we harness its awe-inspiring power and start to make choices about what we want it to do for us.

This chapter is about activating this all-important disciplined behavioural structure; the key to having our financial journey take us wherever we want to go.

Sustainable Finances

Living costs money. It is a fact of modern life. When we have money problems, though, we sometimes persuade ourselves that the fast-track solution to all of our financial woes is to stop spending.

It is a bit like convincing ourselves that the way to lose weight is to stop eating. And whilst this might work for several days, one extreme leads to another and, before we know it, we can quickly be drawn into a pattern of binge behaviour.

If we are to avoid falling into the trap of a 'yoyo budget', we need to embrace our need to spend. Because a disciplined financial structure, in the form of a budget, is nothing if it is not realistic; if it is not sustainable.

The Last Piece in the Puzzle

I think of a budget as being like a jigsaw puzzle made up of 100 pieces. 99 of these pieces represent our overheads and ongoing costs—accommodation, utilities, credit repayments, and so on. The 100th piece is for our living expenses, comprised of grocery shopping, petrol, coffees, take-away food, eating out and, where relevant, cigarettes.

As I have already mentioned, smoking can be listed as a highly-visible separate item of living expenses in our budget, not least because this can act as a powerful incentive to either quit or cut down.

This living expenses piece of the puzzle is one that, more often than not, does not want to fit into the space allocated to it—preferring, instead, to take up the space of several pieces. In fact, the space it does end up occupying can vary erratically from one week to the next. The challenge of any budget, therefore, is to set the size of this most variable piece of the puzzle and ensure that it fits each and every day.

In fact, this piece of the puzzle is like a budget in itself. Just as the state of California, which has one of the largest financial systems in the world, is widely recognised as being an economy within an economy. The effective management of our 'budget within a budget' goes a long way to powering our overall finances towards sustainable success.

The financial journey for some other parts of our budget, such as bills, rent and mortgage, can take place virtually on cruise control, by preprogramming these payments in internet banking. The management of our living expenses, though, needs to be 'in the moment'—in the context of the allowance we have given ourselves as part of our overall budget, that is. Hence the need to walk the walk or 'drive the drive' of this part of our financial journey, so that it remains on track every week.

Just as learning to drive requires motivation and commitment but becomes second nature with time, the same holds true for the management of our living expenses.

The best way to drive this most critical part of our financial plan is to allocate ourselves living expenses on a weekly basis—irrespective of whether our wage gets paid weekly, fortnightly or monthly.

A week encompasses both weekdays and weekends, working days and leisure days, and the associated spread of our financial needs. Also, because our bodies are attuned to a seven-day cycle, adopting a weekly rhythm for our living expenses is something that comes naturally.

By assigning these funds to ourselves on a weekly cycle in our budget, rather than opting for the starvation diet of scrimping and saving from day to day, we are acknowledging the indispensable role that money and spending is going to play on our path to sustainable financial success.

King Cash

Although cash has been around for thousands of years, pundits have been predicting its demise for quite some time now. I can't say how long this trusty old friend will be with us for, but I do know that—like a beloved grandparent—we should treasure and learn from it for as long as we can.

I am not in the business of whingeing about progress. The truth is, though, that plastic cards, electronic transactions and electronic wallets are all one step removed from the real thing.

It is unlikely that modern technology will ever be able to replicate the experience of 'cold hard cash', which has become such a familiar part of our vernacular. Who knows, maybe one day we will regale our astonished grandchildren with seemingly fanciful tales of how we used to hand over paper and metal in return for goods and services.

It is not a question of emptying our piggybanks out at the building society to pay the mortgage every month. But King Cash certainly has the power to keep those potentially unruly living expenses in their place. Not to mention, of course, the mantle of retro-cool that notes and coins are poised to assume in our increasingly ether-based society. Think vinyl records, hand-written letters and paper books. These once unremarkable artefacts have, more recently, taken on an air of defiant nonconformity.

I am reminded of my five-year-old nephew who, upon observing someone manually wind down the window of a decidedly-uncool car, was transfixed by the sight he had just beheld. Having, up to that point in his life, only ever known electric car windows, he could not take his eyes off the rotating handle in question. His look of disbelief and subsequent astonished exclamation of "Awesome!" said it all. He was seriously impressed.

Maybe Gen Z represents cash's best chance of making a come-back. Perhaps they will show up their elders and grasp the fact that cash creates transparency and visibility and comes with a no-surprises guarantee. Although plastic has its place, it renders our day-to-day transactions invisible until, that is, they reappear en masse as unwelcome guests, gatecrashing our latest financial statement.

Debit cards are certainly marketed as being a virtuous form of plastic. In reality, though, they too can reduce the visibility of our daily transactions and have us living in a thick financial fog, wondering what nasty surprise we might bump into next.

By taking the amount that we have already calculated we need for our living expenses out of the ATM as cash once a week and 'parking the plastic', we get to manage our buying decisions in real time—to 'drive our drive' in the here and now. This is step six, the completion of which marks the half-way point on our roadmap to financial success. No more post-electronic-purchase administration and no more focusing on past decisions which, in turn, frees us up to look to, and plan for, the future.

These cash living expenses, which are the 'active ingredient' in our budget, really come into their own when we are away on holiday. This is a time when it is all too easy to throw caution to the wind and then suffer a financial setback as a result. By continuing with a weekly cash routine, we keep control of our money and ensure that nothing can spoil our holiday memories.

Because debit and credit cards tend to act like 'plastic crutches', by becoming dependent upon them, our money-management skills suffer. Kick this dependency, and we can expect to become better at running our finances.

It is a similar phenomenon to the discovery made by the team of scientists at John Hopkins University and the University of Maryland, who found that depriving mice of their sight by keeping them in the dark for a week improved their hearing. It is my experience that depriving ourselves of plastic can deliver correspondingly impressive gains to our financial faculty.

The key to the success of this real-time spending management is the ultimate gift which cash gives us, and that, ironically, is a sense of loss. Every time we hand over a note or a coin we feel, quite rightly, that we are losing something, no matter how small.

This feeling serves to remind us of the finite nature of our money and the fact that every transaction leads to a consequence. Experiencing that consequence, that small sensation of loss, in the here and now—rather than later on, when it is too late—prevents us from being fooled into believing that our funds are infinite and that our current purchase has no bearing on our wider financial situation.

Of course, there are some situations in which it is difficult to avoid the use of a debit or credit card, such as the purchase of a flight ticket. And, in some circumstances, a credit card might offer benefits we wish to take advantage of, such as travel insurance or an extended warranty. In such cases, we simply need to ensure that we make provision for these purchases, such that they fall within, as opposed to outside of, our budget.

In our increasingly-online existence, there might also be some regular purchases that we need to make using a card. If this is the case, it is just a matter of creating these as a separate expense within our budget. If these are food purchases, we can deduct the amount we spend on them from the weekly amount we allow ourselves for living expenses.

By adopting a 'Back-to-The-Future' cash lifestyle as part of our budget, we can have the best of both worlds. As we combine the simplicity and transparency of the Dickensian era with the technology and forecasting power of our own. Neither a cash lifestyle nor the use of technology in isolation is likely to help us to achieve the turn-around we desire. But, together, this is a performance-enhancing combination that places us firmly on the path to success.

Weekly Routine

The day on which we withdraw cash from the ATM quickly becomes a fixture in our weekly calendar. Rather than referring to Monday or Tuesday, for example, we might, instead, find ourselves talking to our partner about 'ATM day'.

And where we do have a partner with whom we share the drive, so to speak, it is important to divide up the 'spoils' with them on that day. Living off cash only works if we plan to avoid being cashless. If one partner in a relationship does find themselves 'without' at the beginning of the cash week, they might have no choice but to reach for the 'not-so-fantastic' plastic in order to get by—the equivalent of a wrong turn on our financial journey.

The rest of the week tends to then fall into line with the rhythm of our cash budget. ATM day or the one after is a good time to do our big weekly grocery shop, for example.

Shopping with cash really does feel different. With our financial week, to a certain extent, contained within our wallet, we start to think harder about how much of the content of that wallet we give away and what for.

Just as the rules and limits that a game of chess impose on us force us to think creatively in order to come out on top, our brains quickly adapt to the new rules of cash living. We start to get creative in order to avoid being 'checkmated' by a lack of funds. We find ourselves picking up an item at the supermarket and asking ourselves whether it is a need or a want and, if it is the latter, replacing it on the shelf. This simple system of real-time categorisation is an incredibly effective way of regulating our financial affairs.

Living off cash also gives rise to the kind of peace of mind that comes from living in a tidy home. And, by continuing our cash existence, our financial system never returns to its previously messy state. Sustainable serenity.

After buying the food, we know how much cash we have to live on for the remaining five or six days. And that is the real advantage of cash. As the week progresses, a cursory glance at the notes in our wallet tells us where we're at. After a while, it becomes as much of a reflex as glancing down at the fuel gauge on a long stretch of highway.

Ideally, the contents of our refrigerator should provide a further clue as to how far into our cash week we are on any given day. Certainly, in the case of a family, the aim is for it to be full at the beginning of the week and virtually empty by the end. Empty is good. It suggests that we have resisted the urge to go on an ad-hoc mission for milk to the local supermarket, only to return with enough groceries to feed the cow that produced it.

The secret of success is to make our financial week predictable to the point of being machine-like. The last day of our cash week might be the day we occasionally treat ourselves to a take-out meal, knowing that we have managed our money sufficiently well over the previous seven days that we can afford it. An achievement that makes any take-away twice as tasty.

Valuing Money

Indeed, the tastiness of this take-away also reveals a deeper truth; the fact that learning to value money does not stop there. Because money is but a means of exchange, we are, in fact, learning to value the things that money can buy; the life that it enables.

Just as learning to value money as a finite resource opens the door to a world of infinite possibilities, this apparently ordinary routine, the mechanism at the core of our financial engine, will take us to extraordinary places on a journey that is anything other than routine.

When ATM day comes around again, if we still have money left over from the previous cash week, we can do with this extra as we please, but we should still withdraw the same amount from the ATM that we do each and every week. Regularity and predictability are the keys to success.

It is amazing just how much value our money begins to take on in the context of this disciplined structure. It only requires a modest surplus at the end of a cash week to make us feel like a millionaire.

That sense of achievement would not have been possible before we began to respect the finite nature of money.

Conversely if, five days into the week, we find that we are virtually running on empty, we need to try to avoid withdrawing any more cash before the next ATM day comes around. The best way to do this is to quickly familiarise ourselves, and make friends, with the contents of our fridge!

Taking Control

In a world that, as we are repeatedly told, is becoming ever more complex, it is amazing how incredibly powerful we start to feel regarding our place in that world when we gain control of our own financial microcosm; our weekly cash living expenses. A fact that is unrelated to whether we are high earners or hard up. It is about the discipline, not the dollars.

When our living expenses start to obey our wishes, it is like being the teacher of the class of the most challenging pupils who suddenly manages to gain the respect of the coolest kids in school. Following that milestone moment, everything else seems to fall into place of its own volition.

Thus, we plot a straight line through our finances, irrespective of the prevailing winds at any given time. All income and outgoings have already been factored into our comprehensive budget to allow for consistent living expenses, which helps to eliminate the highs and lows that might previously have dogged our financial existence. We are no longer tempted to splurge a high account balance or to panic at the sight of a low one. Our behaviour becomes constant, disciplined and predictable, as a result of which our financial system becomes forecastable and compliant to our wishes.

No more drama, just steady progress. No more blaming whatever or whomever for our failure to execute—the high interest of our credit card, our boss for not giving us the overtime, and so on. In fact, the art of assuming uncritical but complete responsibility for our actions enables us to assimilate the skills (by learning from our mistakes) that are necessary to boost our financial engine.

With this emotionally-mature outlook and a well-oiled financial motor to supply the power, we are able to pick a point on the horizon and actually get there. And, thereafter, to choose a spot on the next horizon and arrive there too. At first, we are in disbelief. Everything going to plan. When did that ever happen? After a while, though, we come to accept this as our new, self-created reality.

Far from being too good to be true, as society has taught us that such things must be, it eventually dawns on us that the journey we are now on really is *good* and *true* and *enduring*.

Step 7:

The Stages of Our Journey

Financial Stepping Stones

The wind is in our hair, the sun is shining and we are taking in the sights. Cruising down our very own Route 66 of a financial journey.

We planned our trip, rebuilt our financial engine and hit the road. Now is the time to take stock of where we are and to survey the road ahead.

The Main Street of America or the Mother Road, as Route 66 is also affectionately known, is both a journey from Chicago to Los Angeles and a destination. A trip in the footsteps of cowboys, migrants and pioneers which, once it has been started, makes you feel that you have arrived. Similarly, thanks to our budget, the new way of life we are experiencing is a destination in itself; a place we are happy to be.

Just as the green banks of the Great Lakes, which mark the beginning of this iconic trip, give way to fertile farmland then to barren desert then to Californian beaches, so our own journey unfolds in distinct stages. These are our financial stepping stones, and awareness of them denotes the seventh step on our roadmap to financial success.

Initially, living by a budget is about adopting a more disciplined, rewarding lifestyle and taking control of our finances and, therefore, our life. This might involve extinguishing 'financial fires' from the past so that they can never threaten our economic wellbeing again. This first stage is more about stopping the rot than building anything new. It is also about sowing, rather than reaping.

The tell-tale sign that we have moved to the second stage is that we cease being aware of when we are due to be paid. That is to say, our new system of finances has gained such momentum that we have succeeded in uncoupling ourselves from the payday cycle which we used to follow so slavishly. It is the time when we move from stress*ful* to stress-*free*. Probably the least spectacular but most important financial transition we will ever make. The monetary buffer we have built up, which makes this evolution possible, is the financial equivalent of packing a spare tyre for our journey—making us immune to the effects of any single unexpected bill or emergency.

The tangible results of a budget—the reaping—begin in the third stage. It is when our underlying account balance continues to build. This, in turn, enables us to raise our eyes and extend the reach of our gaze to embrace both the present and the future. It is the time when we begin to see our savings grow and our debt reduce. When we start to walk taller *and* feel that a burden is being lifted.

The fourth stage is to our financial journey what those Californian beaches are to Route 66. When the sustained success of the preceding stage creates a momentum all of its own. It is, to borrow from the Voyager mission, when we go 'interstellar'. When we start taking financial success for granted, but continue to appreciate the life it has enabled. The abundance of our money and the system it operates in have now become a platform for an existence beyond anything we could have planned for.

Transitioning to Success

And though this evolution is entirely positive if, by our nature, we are resistant to change, it might take us some time to accept the reality of the strides we are making. This reluctance to accept progress is a sign that we have become institutionalised by our old financial system, such as it was. A little like Brooks

Hatlen, the elderly prison inmate in the acclaimed film The Shawshank Redemption, who cannot adjust to freedom after half a century of incarceration.

In our case, there are a number of simple but important principles we can adhere to, in order to facilitate this transition and ensure that we are able to progress from one stage of our journey to the next.

The first thing we can do is to persist on our new path. To borrow from the renowned dictum that has been attributed to Calvin Coolidge, the unassuming, no-nonsense, but remarkably-popular 30th president of the United States: "Nothing in this world can take the place of persistence. Talent will not; nothing is more common than unsuccessful people with talent. Genius will not; unrewarded genius is almost a proverb. Education will not; the world is full of educated derelicts. Persistence and determination alone are omnipotent. The slogan 'press on' has solved and will always solve the problem of the human race."

We can, of course, only persist with our new budget if our financial journey is sustainable. Going hard might feel good at the time, but going steady will be more doable over the long term. In the words of Winston Churchill to his chauffeur, "Drive slowly, we're in a hurry."

What's more, we really only need to bring about a small change of direction today in order to be in a whole different place by tomorrow. This is best illustrated by someone who is circumnavigating the Arctic Circle. The tiniest change in direction to the south—a mere one degree, for example—as long as it is sustained, will eventually take them to the equator. From a frozen polar wilderness to the tropics. From one extreme to the other, with a notable lack of intervening drama. Sustained Change of Course + Time = Whole New Destination.

That is why our journey needs to be less about speed and more about direction. Less about monetary progress and more about evolving our underlying habits which will, as a result, deliver the money we need to enable us to achieve the goals we have set ourselves.

Hidden Habits

Just as people associate a budget, in the first instance, with money, rather than behaviour, they also tend to correlate it with the paying down of credit card debt. And though it is an important aim of many personal budgets, this overall objective often masks a wider truth.

An iconic sign at level crossings throughout France reads, "*Un train peut en cacher un autre*" which, translated, means, "One train can hide another." In other words, just because the train in front of us is about to disappear, we should not assume that we are free to cross, as there could be another one on the other side of it.

The train we are currently looking at is our credit card debt. And the other train, or trains, it is hiding are the things the card was being used to pay for.

In order to make progress on our new journey, 'scrapping the plastic' might not be enough. A credit card can hide a multitude of sins and, as per the train analogy, the job is only done once we succeed in kicking the patterns of consumption which are as much the cause of the debt as the use of the credit card itself. Pulling out the weeds is the straightforward part—ensuring we dig up the roots, though, is our ultimate goal.

The chunky but infrequent card acquisitions, such as holidays, certainly stand out on credit statements, but the regular purchases, such as food on the go and eating out, which we make using our credit card, can amount to just as much—if not more—expense. In the same way that anticipation is critical to good driving, it is also the hallmark of any well-run budget. Thinking ahead to avoid such day-to-day expense helps ensure that impulsiveness is replaced with planning.

If we are heading to the beach with the family in summer, for example, it is fair to assume that the kids will be famished after several hours of swimming and playing in the sun. Rather than allowing the fish-and-chip shop across the road to deep-fry a hole in that week's budget, it makes sense to pack a picnic and, in the process, prove that the best things in life really can be free.

In the same way, running out of food at home can be a costly habit. By ensuring that, at the very least, we always have a jar of sauce and a packet of pasta on hand, we can rustle up a cheap family meal quicker than the time it takes to order a pizza.

As well as stocking up on such 'life savers' as part of our weekly shop, if we have children, it is good to make sure we can give them special rewards at home, rather than having to go out. Ice cream is a great example. Instead of an expensive excursion to the local parlour, a treat from the freezer will ensure contented kids and a budget that doesn't go into meltdown.

When planning to go out with children late in the morning, it is worth investing a few minutes to give them a snack or early lunch before leaving, rather than the financial investment that would otherwise be needed to fill their bellies once they are out and about.

If we do want to indulge youngsters while we are out with them, it is difficult to argue with the value of a fast-food soft-serve cone. And by choosing the drive-through option, as parents, we get to control the process, stifle the pester power, and keep junk-food exposure to a minimum.

Awareness and Control

As these examples show, awareness leads to control and, ideally, this positive sequence will repeat itself many times over to propel us through the initial stages of our budget.

We are all familiar with the concept of buying a particular make and model of car that we had considered to be uncommon, only to find that it is, in fact, far more popular than we had first thought. This is obviously because we suddenly become aware of the type of vehicle we have purchased and, as a result, start noticing it just about everywhere. In a similar way, living by a budget and taking control of our money also increases our awareness of the whole of our finances, much of which we had been oblivious to before. In short, we start to see things that had previously flown beneath our financial radar.

The benefit of this process is twofold. Firstly, the fact that our finances are starting to become known to us means the unknown starts to ebb away. As part of this process, our 'fear of the unknown', that was probably reinforced and perpetuated by the myth that 'ignorance is bliss', begins to evaporate. Just as a turbocharger provides an engine with a source of considerable extra power when it is already moving, so this newly-acquired knowledge empowers us on our journey by negating the fear factor that used to restrict the speed of our progress.

Secondly, our increased financial awareness enables us to see and question why we are doing certain things and to decide whether they are beneficial for us.

To take a concrete example in order to illustrate these two points, there is now no reason not to open that credit card bill since, as part of our budget, it no longer belongs in the realm of the unknown and has, therefore, lost its ability to inspire fear. As such, we are empowered to unseal the envelope or to open the PDF on the screen in front of us. This is the first advantage of our new financial awareness.

When we do so, we might notice that we are paying a monthly consumer credit (or payment protection) insurance fee. We are now in a position to take a good, hard look at such extra costs and to ask ourselves whether they are really benefiting us or the credit provider. After having opened the bill, this ability to process and critically assess the facts is the second advantage of our new state of financial awareness.

As in the case of that ubiquitous car model I referred to, it might be that many such arbitrary costs and fees now start to become apparent to us. At first, this can feel overwhelming, especially if we fool ourselves into thinking that we need to address all of these matters today.

The fact that this information is revealing itself to us is, though, a good thing—a sure sign of the 20/20 financial vision that we are managing to cultivate. It is also indicative of a power shift—towards us and away from people who might, in the past, have abused their superior financial knowledge to sell us products that were right for them and their bonuses, but that did not necessarily meet our own needs.

Such examples might include the sky-high interest rate we are paying for the then brand-new car we purchased last year. Or it may be the item—which is doing its best to hide away on our flight receipt—for travel insurance, which we did not even realise we had signed up to when we booked the trip. Or the bill that we receive for an extended warranty on the TV we recently bought, even though this was already provided for by the credit card which we used to make the purchase. Acquisitions that, rather like children's chocolate eggs, each come with a hidden surprise.

Add-on insurances can account for many such surprises. Loosely defined, they are bundled insurance policies that are taken out as part of the acquisition of goods or services, including loans. Generally speaking, they are not what we set out to buy—rather, they are cross-sold to us as part of the sales process.

Consumer credit (or payment protection) insurance is one such example and covers us for circumstances in which we are unable to make credit repayments. When agreeing to this form of add-on insurance, though, there are a number of things we should be aware of.

Firstly, any insurance pay-out goes to the lender, who provides the loan, and not to ourselves, as the consumer.

Secondly, if we already have insurance, such as income protection, consumer credit (or payment protection) insurance might well amount to a wasteful duplication of our existing cover.

Thirdly, such products typically contain a high number of exclusions, meaning that, quite possibly, they were never suitable to begin with—something that often only becomes apparent when we attempt to make a claim and it is too late.

Fourthly, in certain circumstances and jurisdictions, credit law allows consumers to request repayment arrangements of their lenders on the grounds of financial hardship—potentially rendering consumer credit (or payment protection) insurance superfluous.

Finally, it is good practice to try to obtain a comparable quote from an insurance provider other than the provider who is affiliated to the retailer of the goods or services in question.

Thanks to our newfound financial awareness, the unknown has become known, lifting the veil of fear. This 'known' is nothing other than knowledge—information that is power and that is now empowering us to make the right decisions for ourselves. Allowing us to critically assess both existing and potentially-new financial agreements—to our own long-term benefit.

As discerning, confident, assertive consumers, we are no longer easy prey for fellow travellers, with 'free rides for freeloaders' now belonging firmly in the past.

The Democratisation of Personal Finance

Feeling financially knowledgeable, empowered and confident might be new for us. If, at some point in our life, we happen to have been randomly assigned to the 'not-good-with-numbers' box, we have probably—either consciously or otherwise—been living out this self-fulfilling prophecy ever since. Probably by avoiding activities that society categorises as being numbers-based—even though in truth, of course, there are numbers in everything.

For the most part, society's categorisations are, at best, meaningless and, at worst, damaging. It is like someone saying that, because we got into difficulty in water, we are obviously not cut out to swim, so we should not bother learning. Although this statement is absurd, it is far from harmless, insofar as we, as a society, have a tendency to follow such random pronouncements, especially when made by perceived authority figures.

Because it is an accepted truth that anyone who is able, willing and given enough training can swim, we would never label someone as being 'bad with water'.

It is strange, then, just how unquestioningly we accept the damning diagnosis that someone is 'bad with money'. It is as if we were actively wishing the person to 'drown' in their own finances. To describe someone as a novice, on the other hand, implies that the only missing ingredient is the relevant knowledge.

By emphasising what someone *can* do, we democratise the skills associated with personal finance. We take it off its pedestal and put it 'down where it belongs'—on a par with swimming or riding a bike. Personal finance now becomes a gap that can be bridged, a skill that can be learned and a competence that can be mastered by virtually anyone.

This reflects our own development on the current stage of our financial journey. We have overcome any fear that had previously held us back and have become aware of, and knowledgeable about, our personal finances. We have succeeded in demystifying the art of money management and weaving it into the sustainable fabric of our everyday life. We have disproven society's irrational belief that being financially competent is a preordained gift. Achievements that, in effect, now enable us to unlock our inner potential and throw away the key.

Step 8:

Picking Up Speed

Gaining Financial Momentum

The very fact of being on a journey is an incentive to stay on that journey. This is something which became apparent to me when I heard a radio interview with the UK-based American author Lionel Shriver, in which she was discussing Big Brother, her novel about morbid obesity. She made the point that slim people have an incentive to stay slim, because it is desirable to the point of carrying a social status. Being slim, therefore, acts as a motivation to stay slim.

As a result, so the theory goes, the archetypal slim person thinks twice about eating a cupcake. In the event that temptation does get the better of them and they put on weight as a result, they no longer think twice, as they are no longer motivated to stop themselves. And the more cupcakes they eat, the more overweight they become, and the less likely they are to say no to the next cupcake. Why should they?

Whilst this example is intentionally simplistic, it does point to a general truth. That we fight to stay 'in the game'. Once we start to lose, though, our fight has a tendency to desert us. We will move mountains to prevent our finances from slipping into the red. Once there, however, it is all too easy for red to quickly become the new black.

The secret, therefore, is to steer ourselves far away from that 'red zone'. So far, in fact, that the danger it represents ceases to even feature on our journey. In order to do this, a budget has to go from being a novelty to a way of life. From being something we do thoughtfully to something we do without thinking.

Increasing the Momentum

Once the budget is underway, therefore, we need to ask what can be done to increase the momentum that has already started to build. The labour-intensive nature of setting up the budget is over. At the wheel for long stretches of highway, we now have the luxury of time to dream up more efficiencies and turn our reliable financial engine into a high-performance machine. This development, in which waste is eliminated and abundance is created, helps us to move up a gear and take our eighth step on the roadmap to financial success.

As I have already mentioned, as part of a budget, there is no reason not to go out for a coffee again. It might well just change from being a daily ritual—one that we don't quite know if we can afford—to a sometime treat, which we know we can. And, to prevent the occasional caffeine splash from becoming a cash splash, it is a good idea to have a bite to eat before we leave home. That way, we get to enjoy the coffee without the expensive accessories.

If cigarettes form part of our budget's outgoings and we do not feel ready to give up, we might want to try cutting down. One way to do this, assuming we have not done so already, could be to transition to roll-your-owns. Besides being cheaper, they are less convenient and, most people would agree, less enjoyable—both of which can only help if, in the long term, we are looking to quit.

The worst way to burn money is, arguably, the one for which we get very little in return. Parking fines, speeding tickets and penalties for unpaid road tolls can, for some, become a way of life. These then have a habit of leading to a downward spiral of late payment fees, overdrawn bank accounts and, eventually, punitive payday loans.

Living by a budget gives us the incentive we need to issue these habits with a final notice. It is now a matter of managing our behaviour, just as we have started to manage our money. Sticking to the speed limit (perhaps by investing in an in-car GPS with a speeding alarm), keeping to parking times and avoiding tolls where possible are simple measures that can reverse the downward spiral of events remarkably quickly, with our bank balance being the first to benefit.

If late payment fees have become such a fixture of our life that they have started to hang out with our fixed overheads, such as the rent or mortgage repayments, it is time to break up this cosy little clique by sticking to a budget. It is remarkable just how well our cash begins to flow once we have succeeded in shaking off these financial parasites.

Almost as beneficial as stopping the haemorrhaging is getting stuff for free. If there is a choice between parting with cash and going gratis, we need to prioritise the freebies.

A perfect example is joining the local library. It is a win-win. It means we do not spend money on books, we can borrow DVDs for free, and we even get to read the newspaper while we are there. And, nowadays, because we can subscribe to text and email alerts, it is easy to avoid the overdue fines that used to be such a big part of library membership (make that four wins!).

Now that most of our domestic mobile phone calls are no longer billed individually, they are as good as free anyway. It is amazing, though, how many of us still choose to pay to call other countries, when the likes of Skype offer a free alternative. Nowadays, costly international calls make about as much financial sense as traffic fines or late payment fees. Just one more parasitic charge that needs to go away and find another budget to feed off.

On a more general note, it is great to combine 'free' and 'free'; that is to say, in the sense of 'complimentary' and 'liberated'. It is refreshing to remind ourselves that, in the 21st century, money does not need to be a prerequisite to all activity. That leisure does not have to be dominated by consumption. That we are capable of spending time without spending money. Walking or playing in the park, riding a bike, strolling along the beach, swimming in the ocean. These are some of the pleasures of life that, thankfully, money can't buy. It is easy to forget just how readily available such activities are. And, once we experience them again, we find ourselves wondering why we do not do so more often.

Internet shopping may not always be free, but it can come pretty close. If our purchasing patterns have not moved on in the past decade or so, it is probably time to rethink them and to make online a part of our retail mix.

Even if it is just in the form of subscribing to department stores' email newsletters. These are a great way of finding out when sales are on. And, by getting a jump on the competition and being there at the beginning of the sale, we can bag the best bargains for ourselves. This information is particularly valuable when it comes to expensive items and large one-off purchases, like crockery. Also, because such purchases are not usually time-critical, we can afford to wait for that no-brainer deal before making our move.

Before committing ourselves to any big spend, however, it is always wise to 'press pause', step back and ask ourselves two questions. Is this a need, as opposed to a want? And can we afford to pay cash for it? If the answer to both is yes, we can 'press play' and carry on with our plans in the knowledge that we are probably doing the right thing.

Once we are on the budgeting journey, we are on board with the idea of taking a financial haircut. What better way to do this, therefore, than by means of a real-life haircut? Instead of thinking '*salon*', think '*chez vous*'. A mobile hairdresser saves us money and time by coming to our place, instead of the other way around. And we can lop a considerable amount off the family's costs by getting the kids to have a cut at the same time.

Driving can account for a big part of our budget's outgoings. If we have two cars and one is more fuel-efficient than the other, perhaps it can replace the less-economical car for some trips. It is also worth looking at whether four wheels can be swapped for two on any regular journeys. Pedal power is another good example of how healthier finances go hand-in-hand with improved physical wellbeing.

Shopping Shrewdly

Healthy finances can be good for the environment in other ways too. Wasting less food, for example, benefits both our budget and the landfill site that it would otherwise have gone into. One estimate has Australians throwing away up to 20 per cent of the food they buy. This is tantamount to arriving home from the supermarket, opening the car boot and walking one in five bags of groceries straight to the bin. A sobering thought. It is estimated that over a quarter of this wastage comes in the form of leftovers. The equivalent of scraping a huge amount of cash straight off the plate.

As a father of young children, I know that kids—or, should I say, the way we parents feed them—can account for much of this waste. One obvious solution is to feed children smaller portions which, in turn, increases their chances of getting into the desirable habit of eating everything that is in front of them.

Keeping an ongoing shopping list is something that anyone can do. By updating a small chalkboard on the kitchen wall when something runs out, for example, we are less likely to buy too much when we do go grocery shopping.

Meat is one item that is neither great for the bottom or the bottom line. As a child growing up in the 1970s and 1980s, a meal was simply a snack if meat was not on the plate.

Nowadays, though, we have moved on. Society is gradually consuming less animal produce, to the long-term benefit of our health. Meat is transitioning from being a staple to being a treat—from, in many cases, a three-times-a-day basic foodstuff to a once-a-week luxury. A healthier lifestyle which promotes healthier finances by taking the pressure off the budget.

Flour Power

Bread is a staple for most of us, and the range of bread products on offer has evolved over recent years in line with more health-conscious patterns of consumption. As a result, we now have much more choice than back in the white-bread-dominated 1970s. And though continuing to purchase what appear to be slices of cardboard might help our financial health, they will probably do nothing to promote our physical wellbeing. The answer, therefore, might well be to bake our own.

'Saving dough' by baking bread is not a new idea, but it is easier than ever thanks to the advent of affordable, modern bread ovens. With no more 'need' to 'knead', mixing the ingredients is quick and simple, the house smells like home, and we get to choose what goes into our bread.

Preservatives and salt can be kept to a minimum, which is a big plus when we consider that even so-called healthy bread can contain up to four times more salt than is good for us. So whilst the initial motivation might be money, like so many things in life, that is just the beginning.

As a bread-baking convert myself, I calculate that each loaf I bake costs me only half of the price I would be paying in the supermarket. When multiplied by 250 or so loaves a year for my family of five, this adds up to a considerable ongoing annual saving.

For what it's worth, my favourite bread recipe consists of 700ml of wholemeal flour, 350ml of rye flour, three teaspoons of yeast and 500ml of water. By adding 100ml each of linseeds, brown flax seeds, sunflower seeds and pumpkin seeds, the bread takes on more flavour and more bite. And a tablespoon of molasses gives it more taste still and a deeper colour.

So, if you are not doing it already, what are you waiting for? All that is needed is the right recipe, a modest investment in a bread oven and the ingredients.

After that, it's just a matter of using your loaf!

Step 9:

Avoiding Wrong Turns

Preventing Financial Pitfalls

Not long after World War Two, Edward A Murphy Jr, a US air force engineer, conducted experiments to measure the effects on the human body of being propelled at rocket speeds. One unfortunate human guinea pig staggered away, dazed and bloodied, only to be told no data had been collected, as all 16 sensors on his body had been installed the wrong way round.

Murphy then famously observed that, when there is more than one way of doing something, it will be done the wrong way. He was actually suggesting that any process should be designed to be foolproof, such that it could only ever be done the right way. Murphy's Law, though, has come to mean that if something can go wrong, it will go wrong, thereby making poor old Captain Murphy into modern folklore's ultimate pessimist.

Personal finances have a remarkable knack of not going according to plan, with many people ending up, in a financial sense, dazed and bloodied as a result. The statistics say it all. A quarter of American and British families and a third of Australian households have no savings at all. The individuals who form part of these huge groups of people are, potentially, dangerously close to financial hardship.

Murphy's original observation tells us that we have to make the financial system we live by as foolproof as possible. By doing so, we take step nine on our roadmap to financial success and maximise our chances of achieving a positive outcome.

The Credit Card Trap

Often, of course, the successful option is not the most obvious one, and the shiny bright alternative, complete with bells and whistles, cries out to be chosen instead. One such scenario involves running our finances through a rewards credit card—a method of financial management advocated by many in the personal finance industry.

The advantages of this approach, so the reasoning goes, are twofold. Firstly, if we have a mortgage, it enables us to pay the principal of our loan off more quickly and, secondly, we get to maximise the rewards points we earn.

It works by using our credit card to pay for both our living expenses and, also, our regular bills—by having these direct debited from the card. This combined spending is how we earn the rewards points. And, by paying our credit card off in full every month—by means of a direct debit from our main bank account—we make the most of its interest-free days and, thereby, avoid incurring credit card interest.

The heavy use of the card means that, in theory at least, our bank account balance remains largely untouched between credit card repayments. Assuming this healthy bank balance is in an account that is offsetting our home loan, therefore, any given mortgage repayment pays down more of the home loan's principal than would otherwise be the case which, ultimately, leads to the loan getting paid off quicker.

Whilst some people might indeed earn big in terms of rewards points and pay off their home quicker with no side-effects, over the years, I have seen more cases in which this system was a hindrance, rather than a help. The main reason, of course, is that it promotes—wittingly or otherwise—a big-spending, credit card lifestyle, in which it is all too easy to lose track of our actual outgoings.

And because it involves our credit card, to some extent, usurping the role of our bank account, we end up relinquishing a significant level of day-to-day control over our finances, with cash flow forecasting becoming correspondingly more difficult. Living within our means, and even planning to do so, therefore, becomes a challenge. Making this money-management route one which, I would suggest, should not be considered if we are to avoid taking a wrong turn on our journey of financial enlightenment.

The Urge to Sprint

Once we are on this journey and can feel the momentum building, it can be tempting to try to run before we can walk. I have observed that for men, in particular, the initial signs of financial progress can fuel an impatience to achieve even more, even quicker. The mouth-watering prospect of a property purchase being a favourite distraction.

It is as if our old, discredited financial behaviour were trying to make a final come-back by displacing the new. As if our former mentality of instant gratification were attempting to dislodge the responsible, longer-term attitude that is now establishing itself.

A budget really is a marathon, rather than a sprint. And, although it is the victorious 100m sprinter who grabs the headlines at any Olympic Games, the marathon runners cover over 400 times more ground. The rewards of a budget, then, are enormous, but not instant.

Giving the importance of embedding our new-found, forward-looking financial behaviour, it is worth considering the huge capacity that we, as proud owners of a human brain, have for forward-planning. In the 19th century, our comprehension of the brain's power in this regard was crystallised thanks to Phineas Gage, an American railway engineer.

His work entailed breaking up rocks with gun powder, which involved the use of a tamping iron. In an accidental on-the-job explosion, one of these metal rods was propelled in through the left side of his face and out through the top of his head. Even though he did not lose consciousness and did recover from the accident, his friends noticed that he was a changed man.

His new persona was uninhibited, short-tempered and less able to plan. Mr Gage's damaged left frontal lobe, therefore, was instrumental in deepening our understanding of the role played by the frontal lobes of the human brain in general. The stability and sense of perspective, including a capacity to plan for the future, which they bring to our life are qualities that underpin any successful budget.

It might be that we have not made full use of this cerebral ability to 'run our marathon' up to now, but the mental work-out we have already started to give our frontal lobes can only strengthen them. And so, the longer we stay in the race, the stronger they become, and the more able they are to resist the temptation to sprint.

Delaying Gratification

If we have children, it is important that we do all we can to ensure they do not start their 'marathon' by choosing the wrong financial options. The prevalence of intergenerational wrong options was highlighted in a recent report by the Children's Society and the debt charity Step Change. Their findings revealed that over a million British families were struggling with debt and behind on at least one bill.

The benefits of good financial management go far beyond ourselves, far beyond money, and far beyond the here and now. In the same way, the disadvantages of a lack of money harm the lives of our loved ones in ways that reach into all areas of their existence and long into their future. A spokesperson from Step Change concluded that the financial problems they had uncovered were negatively impacting the lives of approximately 2½ million children and that an estimated 20 per cent of children in the UK were being bullied at school because their families were in debt. "And these children are growing up in an environment where they have got low aspirations, low hope for the future. So they're starting the race of life one lap behind."

Our considerable responsibility, as parents, in this key area of our children's development was underscored in another British study, by the government-sponsored Money Advice Service, which found that young people's financial habits were mainly influenced by how their parents dealt with family finances.

In the survey, 1,000 children aged between 15 and 17 were questioned about how they managed their money and, also, whether their families put money aside for unforeseen expenses. According to the research, the children of families in which unexpected costs caused problems—because they were not budgeted for—were less confident with their own money.

Three quarters of the teenagers interviewed said they valued their parents' financial advice above that of financial institutions, friends or teachers, underlining the primacy of our role in determining our children's financial future. A role that, as this investigation shows, is very much about leading by example, in particular, by planning and budgeting for the future.

Children's ability to plan for and consider the future was the focus of a renowned late-twentieth-century Stanford University study, in which young children were offered a range of tempting treats, including marshmallows, from a tray. They were told they could have one treat straightaway or, if they were willing to wait approximately quarter of an hour, they could have two instead.

Scientists followed up the results over a decade later and compared them to the life progress of each participant. They noticed that the children who had chosen to delay gratification coped better with stress, were better at relationships, were healthier and did better academically than those who chose instant gratification.

Interestingly, brain scans of the original participants as adults revealed that the prefrontal cortex (which houses the prefrontal lobes) of the brains of those who had opted to defer gratification were more active than those who had not. Findings that further emphasise the crucial role of this area of the brain in helping us to avoid the temptations of an instant-gratification lifestyle, in favour of the more rewarding outcome of long-term gratification.

Taken together, these studies show that, as parents, whether we like it or not, we are the financial role models our children look up to. If we lead an instant-gratification lifestyle, they will probably do the same. And, by doing so, their quality of life and prospects will almost certainly suffer as a result.

The ability to delay gratification, which is associated with success in so many areas of life, obviously comes more easily to some people than to others. Good habits, though, can be learned. Indeed, in my professional experience, I have witnessed 'instant-gratification junkies' transform themselves into the very best of savers and planners, with the kind of zeal that is the preserve of those who become converted to a particular cause.

Children's behaviour, too, it has been shown, can be adapted by means of a framework of rewards to encourage desired conduct. So, although the 'marshmallow test' gives us fascinating insights, its results are—by no means—set in stone. Leading by positive example by, if we have not already done so, mastering the art of delayed gratification ourselves and implementing an appropriate parenting style can have a transformative effect. This might involve linking at least some element of the payment of pocket money to good behaviour, including the carrying out of chores. By encouraging children's awareness of the future consequences of their current actions, we are able to modify their behaviour for the good and, hopefully, for life.

In essence, delaying gratification is about accepting that we cannot have everything we want right now, even though the availability of easy credit in our society tries to tell us that we can.

By extension, saying no to our children is an important part of living out our financial role-model status and helping them to become delayed gratifiers. When they are with us in the toy shop while we are buying a present for someone else, for example: no, we will not be buying them a gift. When they accompany us to the supermarket: no, we will not be buying them junk food. When they see their friend's electric car and tell us they want one too: no, we do not have enough money to buy them such an expensive accessory. Occasionally, letting children know that money is a scarce resource is fine too.

Rather than perceiving children's persistent nagging in such situations as onerous, we come to view it as a valuable educational opportunity. A chance to increase their ability to defer gratification. To maximise their prospects of leading financially-sustainable lives.

Financial Fuse

One of the most common reasons why people try, but then fail, to live a systemised financial existence is, I believe, that they end up blowing the budget they set themselves. This is often because of the difficulty involved in estimating what they need to live off. As a result, they tend to blame the budget (which might simply be a convenient way of never having to go there again), that is then abandoned in favour of old bad habits.

To address this problem, I recommend, where possible, the inclusion of a 'financial circuit breaker', in the form of an incidentals (or buffer) account, in our budget. Just as a fuse acts to protect an electronic circuit in the event of an unexpected surge in current, so this extra bank account helps safeguard the integrity of the budget in case of an unforeseen surge in outgoings.

It is best to build this into our budget at the same time as we set the amount of our living expenses. This is the time that, having entered our income and expenses into the budget which we are building, we know how much is left over and, therefore, what is affordable.

As a rule, I advise allowing the equivalent of 15 to 20 per cent of weekly living expenses for incidentals. That is to say, paying this amount, over and above the amount we allocate for weekly living expenses, into our incidentals account. I find the best way to do this is to program, on internet banking, a regular transfer of this sum into a dedicated free online savings account. Of course, not every budget will be able to afford this extra expense. If not at the beginning, though, some budgets will be able to accommodate this item in the longer term.

The frequency of such payments could be weekly, on the day following our payday to coincide with our 'ATM day', for example. Or we could pay ourselves this extra sum on a 4-weekly or monthly basis.

Incidentals funds are best defined as deferred living expenses. They are designed to be spent, but not necessarily right now or even this week, for that matter. The aim is to all but forget that we are paying ourselves a regular incidentals allowance. Then, after several weeks, if our car breaks down, our budget will not follow suit, because the necessary funds will be available in our incidentals account.

In my experience, a monthly allocation of incidentals money (on the first of every month, for example) is more effective than a weekly payment. This is because the less-frequent provision of these funds prevents them from becoming a mere extension of our living expenses, as we are then unable to spend them week in and week out. Also, the resulting higher monthly amount is more suited to the chunky expenses which incidentals funds are designed to meet.

Incidentals money is there to ensure that the cost of purchasing presents (although family birthdays and Christmas can be budgeted for separately if finances will allow), leisure activities—such as concert tickets—clothing, shoes, haircuts, unexpected car repairs and unforeseen medical, dental and veterinary treatment are all affordable within our budget.

Although I describe them as deferred living expenses, incidentals funds can also be considered as a form of short-term, targeted savings. Where we can foresee 'lumpy' costs in several months' time, for example, we can save for these by consciously allowing the balance of our incidentals account to grow accordingly over that period.

This also has the imperceptible advantage of getting us into a powerfully-beneficial, short-term savings habit. A regular work-out that firms and tones our savings muscles which, in turn, makes us into highly-trained money managers.

Potentially 'cash-flow-killing' costs that can be neutralised by an incidentals account might come in the form of a glut of otherwise happy occasions, such a baby shower, a wedding and a Mothers' Day meal. The happiness of these events can be short-lived when they become more synonymous with financial fear than effortless enjoyment. Using our incidentals allocation to ensure they turn into the latter rather than the former is what good budgeting is all about: empowering ourselves today to create a successful tomorrow.

The very existence of our incidentals account helps us to bridge the divide between spreadsheet theory and reality. An accomplishment that reduces the chances of a wrong turn on our financial journey. And by ensuring that our children are along for the ride and that no-one is distracted by the empty promises of a shortcut to our desired destination, we take our budget closer to that foolproof nirvana. Something which Edward Murphy would, doubtless, have approved of.

Step 10:

Going It Alone

Personal Budgeting Makes Business Sense

In 1965, John Lennon bought his friend Peter Shotton a supermarket in the south of England so that his childhood pal could run his own business.

This low-risk start-up business model is, unfortunately, only open to the select few lucky enough to count generous rock stars among their close friends.

Other would-be entrepreneurs live or die by their own endeavours. And that, let's be honest, is the appealing part of going into business. The element of risk, the ability to fail, the fact that nothing is guaranteed. Only in this uncertain context can success taste so sweet and be so worth striving for.

So, whereas many people would probably envy the chance that Peter Shotton was given, most dyed-in-the-wool entrepreneurs would not. They would want to succeed on their own two feet, rather than on the shoulders of a rich patron.

This chapter is aimed at small business owners, as well as those who are planning on, or open to, going into business. In short, it is for anyone who is treading their own path on this financial journey.

In truth, though, many of the challenges facing business proprietors are similar to the pitfalls that confront wage earners (albeit, usually, on a different scale). As such, much of this subject matter will have a universal relevance.

This tenth step on the roadmap to financial success outlines why we do not need a wealthy benefactor to help us to reduce risk and increase certainty. How, instead, we can achieve this ourselves by living within a budget and forecasting our cash flow.

It's Personal

Talking about personal and business finances in the same breath can feel like breaking a hushed taboo. Enshrined in orthodox thinking is the fact that the two should be autonomous, just as the separation of church and state is such a hallowed part of many national constitutions.

This accepted rationale, though, relates very much to banking arrangements since, for both fiscal and practical reasons, it certainly makes sense to have a dedicated bank account for personal finances and another earmarked for business.

Beyond that, however, it is fair to say that any small business is very personal. If we are in either the start-up or the establishment phase of a business, it is often akin to having another mouth to feed. It is likely to be a drain on our personal finances for quite some time before it starts to contribute. And, as with any new family member, the outgoings are sure to begin well before the business comes into existence.

Intimately bound up, as it is, with our personal lives, the costs associated with a fledgling business which is dependent upon our financial support need to be factored into our personal budget right from its conception.

Although a business plan and business cash flow forecast are standard cornerstones of any new venture, especially where business borrowing is involved, such comprehensive planning is almost never replicated in the area of our personal finances. The lack of any personal budgeting component is, I would argue, a glaring omission from our start-up project and leads us to making crucial early-stage decisions with less than the full facts at our disposal.

By the time we find ourselves with our 'new baby', because there is unlikely to be any personal budget in place, we default to the infamous tried, tested but still-unproven 'muddle-along' plan. And the more time the 'new addition' to our life takes up, the less likely we are to get around to putting a personal budget in place.

Adherents of the muddle-along plan live the dream day by day, rather than planning in advance *how* to live the dream. Rather than imposing a structure on events, such that they culminate in the dream. Rather than controlling everything within their sphere of influence to make the dream happen.

The fact is that personal finances which work in harmony with, as opposed to separate from, business finances are usually the most powerful weapon in our armoury to ensure that the business achieves its full potential.

The earliest form of manual gearbox transmission was invented at the end of the 19th century. Back then, timing and throttle control were everything when 'shifting' gears by sliding them along their shafts. If the gears were not rotating at the same speed, the teeth would fail to mesh with one another. Given the crunching soundtrack that frequently accompanied these engine manoeuvres, it is little wonder that they came to be known as crash boxes.

If, as entrepreneurs, we fool ourselves into thinking we can afford to invest time in our business at the expense of our personal finances the two, inevitably, will not work in harmony with one another. Such a lack of coordination invariably leads to a crash box-like financial relationship between them—one that is similarly discordant and jarring.

Then, when the time does come for the business to 'move up a gear', it is unlikely to be able to do so if our personal finances are not working in sync with the business, leaving our business finances to overheat. In this situation, the 'high-revving' financial engine of our business cannot be sustained, and our dream eventually mutates into the nightmare of another failed new business. All for the want of a systemised arrangement of personal finances.

Entrepreneurial Extremes

As business owners, we have significantly more freedom than our employee counterparts. Freedom to make a go of things, and freedom to make a hash of them. Freedom to become dazzlingly rich, and freedom to become dirt poor. As the self-appointed head of our own little kingdom, our life lacks the kind of structure that is imposed on our fellow citizens. And neither is our behaviour subject to the same checks and balances.

Very few lives are lived in a vacuum, but a self-employed life can come pretty close. Whereas accountability and feedback are all-too-familiar elements of any employee's key performance indicators, as business owners, we have the ability to conveniently side-step any unpleasant truths. One of which might well be the parlous state of our personal finances. It might, of course, be that such financial problems lie in the future, as opposed to the present, which is something we are probably unaware of, if we have no system to predict that future. In any case, we can always appease ourselves with the hope of increased future business turnover as the panacea for any financial ills.

The feast-and-famine aspect of many small businesses' finances certainly lends itself to an over-dependency on the proverbial bumper crop which is just weeks away. And our tendency, as small business owners, to treat such high periods of business revenue as windfalls that are somehow separate from other business income is where we can easily come unstuck.

If, for example, a record financial harvest is in the offing, it is all too common for us to allocate its spoils well in advance of the event itself. With the subtext being that these proceeds are unconnected with the business's underlying finances and are, therefore, 'cream on top' which can be assigned, at will, to pet causes.

When we live by a personal budget, we start to view our personal finances in a much more holistic way. One lot of personal income minus one lot of personal expenses giving rise, over time, to one lot of personal cash flow. This 'money mindset' then gives us a deeper understanding of the way all of our finances work, including those of our commercial operation, as any business budget will reveal. One batch of business revenue minus one batch of business outgoings leading to one batch of business cash flow.

Peter and Paul

To see it any other way usually involves unwittingly inviting our not-so-good friends Peter and Paul into our life.

The phrase 'robbing Peter to pay Paul' signifies the act of neglecting to pay one entity in order to be able to pay another. It is thought to have originated some 500 years ago, before the English Reformation; that is to say, before the Church of England broke away from the Catholic Church, in the 16th century. At that time, Catholic taxes were levied by both St Peter's Church in Rome (the Vatican) and St Paul's Church in London. By omitting to pay the Peter tax in order to be able to afford the local Paul tax, one was robbing Peter to pay Paul.

When we do inadvertently invite Peter and Paul to the party, we probably do not realise, for quite a while, that they are milling around among the guests. Once they make their presence felt, though, we soon start to ask ourselves whether these unwelcome interlopers will ever leave.

Typically, the issuing of an unintentional invitation to this dastardly duo involves debt or the taxman or, heaven forbid, both.

It might all start with the mouth-watering prospect of an apparent business windfall, which leaves us itching to get our hands on it. There is an undeniable satisfaction in planning to pay off in full that maxed-out personal credit card which has been haunting our finances for some time now.

Neutralising the irksome card in isolation, though, is like setting out to take our opponent's queen at all costs and disregarding the 31 other pieces on the chessboard. A move that is bound to catch us out before too long.

As with so many enduring double-acts, the individual personalities of our unwanted visitors are quite distinct but, ultimately, perfectly complementary.

According to the saying, Paul is the one we pay. In the credit card scenario I refer to, Paul plays the role of the card provider to perfection. He is the extrovert of the pair. The one who could sell anything to anyone. As borne out by the aforementioned scene, in which he did a wonderful job of relieving us of what appeared to be a business bonanza by successfully promoting the aspiration of a balance-free credit card to the exclusion of all else.

And, like any good sales person, he even managed to create in us a feel-good association with the handing over of this cash. We can only marvel at such a bravura display.

Peter, so the saying goes, is the one we are not able to pay, because we have paid Paul. Peter is the more subtle of the two. He is the introvert who, nonetheless, always steals the show and receives a standing ovation at the end of each nuanced performance.

He is at home in the shadows, and anonymity is his trump card. In fact, when we handed over the proceeds to Paul (the credit card provider) in the preceding scene, Peter's presence was almost ghost-like. But he was there. We did not know it at the time, but Peter was the taxman, looking on from the side of the stage.

Peter (the taxman) had a vested interest in doing so, because he knew he was being 'robbed'. He knew that Paul's payday was his zero sum game further down the line.

By the time the stage hand indicates to Peter (the taxman) and ourselves that our joint scene is finally upon us, we do not need to dig too deep to portray the emotional anguish caused by our inability to pay Peter his dues, as the pain we feel is all too real and all too raw.

Unfortunately, however, we fail to grasp that this scene was actually caused by our previous appearance with Paul (the credit card provider). Unable, as we are, to join the dots and relate the contents of one scene with another, we remain ignorant of the fact that our failure to pay Peter (the taxman) was triggered by our overpayment to Paul (the credit card provider). And, so, our regular scenes with Peter and Paul carry on as before, and our debts with the former become increasingly onerous.

Until, that is, the penny (if we still have one) drops, and we start to 'get it'. To get the fact that our business revenue is all one, as are our business outgoings. To get the fact that a short period of high business income should not be treated as a jackpot but, instead, needs to be seen in a longer-term context. To get the fact that our own actions have been perpetuating Peter and Paul's unwelcome presence in our life.

The characters in this play are interchangeable with a whole range of other individuals. Paul does not have to be a credit card provider. He could be any creditor or service provider we pay too much money to without regard to Peter, whoever he may be.

And if, as business owners, we make the common mistake of spending pre-tax business receipts as if they were post-tax income, Paul (the credit card provider in the previous scenario) could be literally anyone—anybody, that is, to whom we pay this pre-tax business revenue. A situation in which we will always end up having to account for ourselves to Peter, the taxman.

Hence, it is imperative that we put the right amount of tax (including any relevant consumption tax) aside on a continuing basis, in order to ensure we are not spending 'funny money'. Otherwise, in the inevitable subsequent meeting with Peter, the taxman, he will be unlikely to see the humorous side.

Any long and worthwhile journey involves making mistakes along the way. They even make for a more interesting trip. The most important thing on our financial journey, though, is that, at some point or other, we learn from them. Even if this does not happen after the first or the second or even the third such misstep, we do need take personal responsibility and apply the lessons we have learned eventually. In order not to repeat them forevermore. In order, in this case, not to replay our regular scenes with Peter and Paul. In order for them to finally exit the stage for good.

A Business-Friendly Personal Budget

Counterintuitive though it may be, the first step in achieving this business turnaround is to start with the personal, by drawing up a comprehensive personal budget, in the form of a personal cash flow forecast. This will give us a priceless piece of information; namely, the amount we need to earn from the business.

As employees, the starting point of this process is income—dependable and predictable as it usually is—followed by outgoings. As business owners, though, it is usually best to work the other way around.

If we are *aspiring* business owners, it makes sense to delay turning off our wage-income tap for as long as possible while we get our business up and running. Often, though, it is not logistically possible to continue our day job *and* run our new enterprise, in which case, we have to forego these earnings in order to start the business.

Because our new business income tends to be anything but reliable, and precisely because our outgoings are now likely to be the most consistent part of our finances, it is advisable to start by inputting our personal expenditure, including both living expenses (in the form of groceries, etc) and bills. These outgoings should also include any investments that we need to make in our business, according to the information contained within our business cash flow forecast—assuming, of course, that we have one.

Having keyed in these costs, if there is any non-business revenue, such as a second wage or welfare payments, we should be sure to enter these net amounts in the income section of our budget.

We can then subtract our forecast personal outgoings from our forecast net personal income (second wage, etc). The resulting cash flow forecast, if it is in deficit, will show how much the business needs to contribute to the net income in our budget, and by when, in order to keep our personal finances afloat.

A 'Personal-Friendly' Business Budget

Once we know how much we need to earn from the business, it then only remains to work out if this is feasible. And the way to do this is by means of an accurate, thorough and realistic business cash flow forecast.

This might involve building one from scratch. Or it might be a case of brushing the 'digital dust' off the business cash flow forecast that has been sitting, unopened, on our hard drive ever since we used it to apply for a business loan with the bank.

If the verdict is that the business is in a position to plug our projected income gap, in consultation with our accountant or bookkeeper, we can build a schedule of regular business drawings or business wage payments, which will be revenue for our personal budget. So that we know, for example, how much the business is required to contribute every week for the next year in order to support our personal finances.

This proactive schedule of planned payments from the business also helps us to avoid the scenario, so prevalent among those who are self-employed, of reactive, ad-hoc payments from the business account, and the chaos that usually accompanies them. Such an arrangement of systemised payments is just one example of the formidable extra power that can be harnessed when our two financial engines are working in unison.

If, however, it transpires that the business will be unable to give us the income we need, we will have to implement a mid-journey change of plan. Rather than regretting the decision to have gone into business in the first place, it is a matter of taking a 'glass-half-full' approach, by recognising that our newly-interconnected personal and business budgets are empowering us in the present to minimise or avoid losses in the future. Providing us with the opportunity to ensure long-term financial viability.

In the worst-case scenario, this change of plan could involve getting out of the business altogether. It might well, though, come down to the need to increase the future revenue in our personal budget by, for a while at least, going back to work part-time. If so, it is important not to overcommit ourselves, as small businesses have an uncanny knack of soaking up much of our time.

No-one, to paraphrase John Lennon, wants to end up working 'Eight Days a Week'.

Step 11:

Filling the Tank

Boosting our Income

My grandfather had the gift of the gab. With his Irish accent, he could charm the birds off the trees. And his repertoire of wit and wisdom could rise to any occasion.

A particularly harsh air current, for example, would be labelled 'a lazy wind' as, he explained, it would cut straight through you, rather than making the effort to go around you.

Another of his pearls of wisdom was the fact that, although most people are hung up about what they earn, the amount they spend plays a central role in determining how well off they are.

As a young boy, I listened intently, but lacked the life experience to venture an opinion. Now, years later, I often find myself thinking back to his shrewd insight, since much of my professional life is spent helping people to become better off by gaining control of their spending.

Spending versus Income

Our spending is, without doubt, much easier to influence than our income, which makes it a logical lever to pull in order to establish control over our finances as a whole. And, though my late grandfather's observation was certainly pertinent, experience now tells me that this emphasis on our pattern of spending should not be to the exclusion of the revenue component of our personal budget.

Occasionally, irrespective of how much discipline we impose on our spending, we find that there is no way around the necessity to increase what we earn, either temporarily or permanently, in order to ensure a long-term, viable budget. This is the eleventh of the 12 steps on our roadmap to financial success. Often, driving carefully will ensure that the fuel in the tank will get us where we need to be. Sometimes, though, there is no denying the need to fill up at the pump on our financial journey.

It is usually only possible to confidently conclude that increased income is necessary after we have put a budget in place and established control over our outgoings. After having dealt with our spending, we can be sure that we have done all we can to make savings and, thereby, to reduce our income deficit. By then, we can also be confident in the knowledge that the extra income we need will not be used to finance wasteful spending. Indeed, we can rest assured that any future increases in income will be so much more productive than they would otherwise have been.

In the context of our budget, we are now able to put a number on the revenue deficit that we need to make up. A well-defined goal that our financial engine will help us to reach.

Raising Revenue

If we have established that it is the income side of our personal ledger which now requires our attention, we need to be open to the various forms that any revenue-boosting solutions might take.

The obvious place to start is with our current income. If we are due a pay-rise, the answer to our problems could already be in the pipeline.

If not, we might need to look at other ways of boosting our existing earnings. By making ourselves available for extra shifts or overtime. By redoubling our efforts to hit our sales targets and earn extra commission. By ensuring we hit our key performance indicators, in order to earn a bonus.

Right now, our bonus is, in reality, more of a necessity than a luxury—something that is undoubtedly spoken for well ahead of time. As we progress through the stages of our budget, though, it will revert to its true definition and become the added extra that it is meant to be. By protecting such surplus income and making it highly visible and tangible, a budget addresses one of the almost ubiquitous financial complaints of all—that of having nothing to show for one's endeavours.

Living by a budget incentivises us like nothing else can. As a forecasting mechanism that enumerates the potential rewards of improved financial performance, including bonuses that we actually get to keep, it is the proverbial 'carrot'. As a transparent system that quantifies our financial pain in numbers that are difficult to dispute, it is also the 'stick'.

If extracting more from our existing source of income is not a possibility, we may have to look to options that lie beyond our current horizons. To a change of employer, for example, if this would increase our earnings. To a more highly-paid career assuming, that is, that the investment of time and money in any relevant upskilling would be feasible and worthwhile as part of our budget. Or to a second job. Indeed, this might be the quickest—and, therefore, the most viable—way to open up the money tap.

If our day job is literally just that, it could be a case of taking on something which involves working evenings and, perhaps, weekends too. Such a move often entails work for which we are overqualified and which, therefore, is likely to be unappealing. The attraction lies not in the work itself but, rather, in the silver lining that this second income gives to our financial cloud. It all comes back to the financial incentive which runs right through our budget.

And because the time dimension of the budget is second only to the monetary one, our cash flow forecast might tell us that the need for extra income is only temporary. If this is the case, having an end-date in sight can further motivate us to take the plunge and commit to a second job, even though it is beneath our abilities. A pre-planned exit strategy can certainly ease our entry into an otherwise unattractive situation.

If we have a partner who does not currently work but who is able and willing do so, this could be a painless way of creating a much-needed second income. And, even if it is only in the form of a part-time job, the positive effect that this has on our overall cash flow is usually out of proportion to its actual amount. This is because these additional funds will probably not all be used to service our ongoing costs (most of which are already being met by our existing income), making this extra revenue stream an extremely valuable one.

The easiest way to illustrate just how beneficial even a small second income can be is to compare our current borrowing power, based on one wage, with our capacity to borrow based on two. An online home loan calculator will usually reveal a surprising and substantial difference between the two scenarios.

Thinking Laterally

Assuming that our budget's income does have to be increased, we might need to broaden our definition of 'income' to ensure the success of our revenue-raising exercise. By, for example, monetising a particular skill we have, in order to supplement our regular earnings—subject, of course, to any relevant legal, compliance and insurance considerations. In the case of a hobby pianist, giving music lessons. For someone who is gifted at practical work, carrying out property maintenance. Regarding a person with a talent for IT, building websites, and so on.

Such flexibility and versatility are, in any case, proving to be increasingly common requirements of an ever-more-competitive workforce.

These kind of forays into unchartered professional waters can provide us with a valuable 'overdrive' option on our financial journey. Occasionally, they can even lead to a permanent change of gear, in the guise of a life-enhancing career transformation. A modicum of courage is certainly called for but, having already taken our finances by the scruff of the neck, we have more than proven our ability to go above and beyond in the pursuit of success.

Our understanding of what constitutes income might even need to be widened to include revenue that is not a payment for work. This might come in the form of money from parents, for example. An offer to pay for our children's new shoes. A willingness to replace our old car. Not everyone is lucky enough to be the focus of such largesse. And not everyone who is, is willing to accept it, even though it could be a financial lifeline.

If we fall into the latter category and pride is preventing us from accepting what is on offer, it might just be a matter of knowing where we are in our financial cycle and what lies ahead. In the first stage, we sow. In the second, we go from stressful to stress-free. In the third, we reap. And in the fourth, we go interstellar.

In the first stage, we usually need all the fuel we can get in order to power our way to the successive stages of our financial journey. And if, in this initial phase, we are able to see from our cash flow forecast when the third stage will be, we might be more inclined to accept any family generosity, knowing when we will be able to afford to pay it back. This could involve programming a future repayment into our budget as an unexpected 'thank you' to the family member concerned.

If there are any welfare payments that we are entitled to but which we are not currently claiming, this is something we need to get onto. Again, assuming we can foresee the reaping stage of our budget, these are not payments that we might qualify for, or need, in the future. But, by asserting our right to them now, we will be increasing the chances of our budget plan becoming reality and, by extension, decreasing the likelihood of being a burden on the welfare state in the long term.

It might even be feasible to supply this extra financial fuel ourselves—by selling some of our stuff which, thanks to the internet, has become a universally-accepted way of boosting income. As well as the big established websites, there are now ever-more community-based websites and apps which cater for local sales. The fact that they serve a geographically-targetted clientele often cuts out the need for shipping, making transactions quicker, easier and less expensive for the vendor.

Bringing money in and getting stuff out is a win-win. It is part of the wider lifestyle makeover that living by a budget involves. Healthy, simplified, flowing finances which are mirrored in every area of our life. This process helps us to free up, and feel good about, our physical surroundings in the same way as we appreciate our new financial circumstances.

Having established and experienced the ramifications of our level of income, it is incumbent upon us to share this newfound wisdom with our children once they start to give serious consideration to their own career options. This includes letting them know about the likely remuneration of a given occupation and how this could impact their financial future and the life choices that will be open to them.

Of course, this is not about making them choose the best-paid professions and reject the most poorly-paid jobs. It is simply about helping them to make the right choices by having all the facts, including the relevant financial information, at their disposal.

In his own way, I guess that is what my grandfather was doing for me. Giving me the benefit of his 'distilled Irish wisdom' for my own future. In which case, I can honestly say that it had its desired effect. If I listen hard enough, I can make out the words, "I told you so", delivered in a mischievous Irish accent.

Yes, you most certainly did!

Step 12:

"Oh, the Places You'll Go!"

The Life your Budget Will Help you Create

"Congratulations!
Today is your day.
You're off to Great Places!
You're off and away!"
         (Dr Seuss)

America in 1977.
The year in which the world's first personal computer takes the Consumer Electronics Show in Chicago by storm.

Five years after NASA unveiled the Space Shuttle, *Enterprise* becomes airborne for the first time, at Edwards Air force Base, atop a Boeing 747.

The phenomenon of Star Wars is unleashed, to the fanfare of its iconic motion picture film score, on the inhabitants of Planet Earth.

Fleetwood Mac releases its now-legendary Rumours album, which will become one of the best-selling records in history.

By August, Grease, which will go on to be one of the most enduring film musicals of all time, is being shot in studios and high schools in southern California.

Meanwhile in Nashville, Tennessee, just weeks after performing his last-ever concert, in Indiana's Market Square Arena, Indianapolis, Elvis Presley dies at his Graceland home at the age of 42.

This is the setting in which Voyagers 1 and 2, the inspiration for our own breakout financial and life-changing journey, blast off into space in the late summer of 1977.

New Frontier

Fast forward 35 years and nearly 19 billion kilometres. The two spacecraft remain in daily contact with NASA's Deep Space Network, whose ultra-sensitive antennas capture a signal which, travelling at the speed of light, takes around 17 hours to reach Earth, from a transmitter that is comparable in strength to a refrigerator light bulb, at a power level that is 20 billion times less than that of a digital watch.

On Thursday September 12, 2012, thanks to these remarkable antennas, it is confirmed that humanity's most distant object, in the form of Voyager 1, has traversed the outer boundary of our solar system and entered interstellar space. The first human-made thing ever to do so. An achievement described by NASA as being comparable in importance with the first circumnavigation of the earth nearly 500 years previously and the first footprint on the moon nearly half a century earlier.

This unassuming probe which, like its sister ship, was strapped to a Titan-Centaur rocket to lift it beyond the earth's gravitational pull, has since started to slip beyond the reach of even the sun. By leaving the heliosphere, the massive bubble of magnetic fields and charged particles that our star chooses to surround itself with, it has departed the 'sun kingdom'.

In doing so, our plucky little protagonist has altered our understanding of our planetary system and beyond. It now finds itself travelling through cold galactic plasma, 40 times denser than its outer-solar equivalent, with the sun's wind yielding to the breeze of the stars.

If it hasn't already happened, today could mark the beginning of our very own mission. The day on which we finally resolve to take control of that most powerful engine of our life, our money. A day that, in years to come, will stand tall among all of the life-enhancing events of our personal narrative. Just as, decades on, the afterglow of the departure of the Voyager twins from their launch site in Florida continues to illuminate the skies of our imagination.

Embracing the Unknown

As the Voyager example shows, modest beginnings in no way preclude a spectacular operation. Making a start, therefore, is all-important.

And although our goals form a critical part of our mission, we need to be open to experiences that go beyond our current imaginings. As Voyager 1 chief scientist, Ed Stone, puts it, "…Voyager has taught us… the most important thing we will learn is that which we didn't know we would learn."

It is reassuring to hear that, even with a level of preparation as detailed as NASA's, it is not possible to plan the mystery out of a mission.

Ambitious goals certainly make a mission worthwhile, but unexpected discoveries—which, unlike goals, cannot be planned—give it a depth, richness and value that go far beyond any human scheme.

Just like the Voyager spacecraft, our systemised personal finances are a vehicle. One that allows us to escape from what Dr Seuss describes as "…a most useless place", where "Everyone is just waiting." A mechanism that makes the ensuing journey possible.

This vehicle, therefore, has its place and its limits. There are, however, no limits to what it can help us to achieve. The vehicle is the 'known', which lifts the veil from the unknown. Which, in the case of Voyager 1, for example, enables cosmic currents to join solar winds in the annals of our wider human experience.

Embracing the unknown, that which lies beyond the plan—unsettling though this can be—is the key to inviting this new dimension of experience into our life.

If we are loathe to welcome the unfamiliar into our world, it is probably because we are not yet sufficiently dissatisfied with the familiar. We probably just need more time to experience the uselessness of that 'Waiting Place'. Once we do reach the required level of dissatisfaction, though, we will be ready to escape to the 'bright places' of Dr Seuss's celebrated story.

It can, of course, never be all plain sailing, hence his entreaty to "…hike far and face up to your problems whatever they are."

In fact, the point at which we do not think we are achieving anything worthwhile on our own financial journey often turns out, in hindsight, to be just the moment that we were forging ahead. By the time NASA grasped that Voyager 1 had left our solar system, over two weeks had passed. It was only once the data was analysed, on September 12, that they realised—by means of reverse extrapolation of the statistics—that one of humanity's most stunning feats had, in fact, already taken place, on around August 25.

This was momentous. The mission now found itself in territory that was 'off the scale' of its original objectives. The rules of the game had changed, and Voyager's potential was now, at once, unlimited and unknown.

Achieving the Unthinkable

With the vast distance that now lies between this probe and Planet Earth, the link between 21st-century interstellar space and that late summer in late 1970s America seems so tenuous as to be barely believable. It is almost as if Voyager 1 were never really of this world. A perception which was accentuated by the last eerie snapshot it took of its home planet, some quarter of a century ago, in which—then 'only' 6 billion kilometres away—the earth already appeared as a tiny dot, a mere fraction of a pixel, suspended in the endless darkness of deep space.

The truth is, though, that Voyager is very much of this earth. And it is precisely this combination of humble beginnings and extraordinary achievements which touches, inspires and motivates. Encouraging us to reach ever higher on our own financial journey, to steer our life into hitherto undreamt-of realms and, in doing so, to take the final, liberating step on our roadmap to financial success.

The modest initial mission is something most of us can relate to. The momentum which then builds makes conceivable what was previously inconceivable. In Voyager's case, the exploration of all of Earth's giant outer-planetary neighbours, 49 moons and a domain beyond the solar system, one exciting new frontier at a time.

In preparation for our own journey, we need to strap ourselves in and be ready to enter terrain that bears no resemblance to our familiar financial surroundings. That does not even feature on our initial roadmap. That transcends anything we can imagine from our current vantage point. A new world of possibilities once we reach the horizon of financial control, beyond which all routes lead to opportunity.

The fact that Voyager is about becoming everything it is possible to be is reflected in her payload. A gold-plated audio-visual disc with messages from the folks back home in 50 languages, and pictures to match. Who knows how another intelligent life form might one day perceive the sound of Mozart or Chuck Berry, or waves breaking on a beach or a baby crying. But it is all there in simultaneously matter-of-fact and moving detail.

In their understated way, these two low-budget 1970s Americans represent the best of humanity. And they extend an invitation to us to become all that we can be, to surpass our expectations of ourselves and, in doing so, to make our own gold-plated contribution to our universe.

"you're off to Great Places!
Today is your day!
Your mountain is waiting.
So...*get on your way!*"
        (Dr Seuss)

www.ingramcontent.com/pod-product-compliance
Lightning Source LLC
Chambersburg PA
CBHW051533170526
45165CB00002B/716